Butterflies

and tales of the Bizarre

by

David Lewis Paget

BARR BOOKS

For my friends at the Dinosaurs Club
The Copper Triangle Writers Group
For your fellowship
And your coffee

Other Poetry available by the author:

Pen & Ink – The Complete Works 1968-2008
Timepieces – The Narrative Poetry
At Journey's End – The Narrative Poetry, Vol. II
The Demon Horse on the Carousel – and Other Gothic Delights
Poems of Myth & Scare
The Devil on the Tree – and Other Poems of Dysfunction
Tales from the Magi
Taking Root
The Storm and the Tall Ship Pier
The Book on the Topmost Shelf
Tall Tales for Tired Times
The Season of the Witch
Smugglers Pie
My China – Poetry in and about China
The Red Knight – Selected Poems

All Poems
Copyright © 2014-2015
By David Lewis Paget
ISBN - 978-0-9750856-9-1
All Rights Reserved

Foreword

Poetry! Inspiration or perspiration? A little of each I think, as I launch this, the eleventh book of narrative poems written since 2006. Initially inspired by the writings of the 18th and 19th century classical poets after over thirty years of writing introspective poems, I began to realise that these were just contemporary froth as far as literature was concerned. The heavy stayers were narratives, poems that would live on down the centuries because they dealt with stories about the human condition, and were entertaining fictions. Coleridge and Poe, Blake and Noyes, these were my mentors. The macabre and gothic became natural themes for me, being a Scorpio by sign, and an introvert by nature.

However, there has been a mellowing as time progresses; perhaps that's a function of age. In this latest collection there is less emphasis on blood and gore than in the past, as my regular readers will recognise. The themes and plots become more subtle, the characters softer and more introspective themselves, the challenges they face more psychological than physical as my own physicality fades into the past.

The beauty and simplicity of the English language is my prime focus, because that is what induced me to write poetry in the first place. To savour the rhythms here, read slowly, and give these poems sufficient time to reside in your subconscious. You won't be sorry you did.

David Lewis Paget   March 2015

Contents

Index of First Lines   **159**

1. Butterflies — 7
2. Before Trafalgar — 9
3. If I Thought… — 11
4. The Devil is in the Detail — 13
5. The Threat of the Weaker Sex — 16
6. The Wizard of Did! — 18
7. Wrong Mountain! — 20
8. Only the View — 22
9. Bell, Book & Candle — 24
10. The Shadow Makers — 27
11. Crimson Dawn — 29
12. Bad Christmas — 31
13. The Guilt Trip — 33
14. What Happens? — 35
15. Nadine — 36
16. The Tale on a Bloodied Screed — 39
17. Two Paths — 42
18. Dead Man's Eyes — 44
19. The Call of the Sea — 47
20. The Wages of Sin — 51
21. Auto-da-fé — 53
22. Hadron Hell — 56
23. Photographs — 58
24. The Phantom Bus — 60
25. Powerless! — 62
26. Threatening Rain — 65
27. The Temptation — 67
28. Table Tapping — 69
29. The Midnight Plane — 71
30. The Beat of the Drum — 74

31. Monsters!	77
32. Talking Heads	80
33. Never Come Here Again!	83
34. The Duke of Spur	85
35. The Bed & the Wardrobe	88
36. Girl on a Train	91
37. McAvanagh's Hill	93
38. The Naked Lady of Houghton Hall	96
38. The Watcher	99
39. Jonathon's Dilemma	101
40. Gulp! – (Lol)	103
41. The Gargoyle	105
42. In A Poem's Wake	108
43. Double Jeopardy	110
44. To Bed! To Bed!	113
45. The Blank Page	116
46. The Reversal	118
47. In Search of the Woman Thing	120
48. The Cuckoo's Nest	123
49. The Witch of Willow Vale	126
50. An Old Love	129
51. The Grotto	130
52. The Egg	133
53. The Non-Event	136
54. The Wake	138
55. Thicker than Water	139
57. The Girl with a Deadly Charm	141
58. The Village that Lived in the Sky	143
59. Return of the Wanderer	144
60. I Wish I Could Be Like You!	146
61. The Fisherman	149
62. Goodbye!	151
63. The Horror Tales of the Greats	153
64. The Landslide	155

Butterflies

She asked me how she had come to me
On a sunny afternoon,
She couldn't remember anything,
Her memories had flown.
She looked in awe at the dress she wore
And the sparkles on her shoes,
'I didn't have any of these before,
But what have I got to lose?'

I had her in mind for a Faery Queen
Or maybe a party girl,
I hadn't a plot to fit right then
But thought I'd give her a whirl.
She had such grace and a lovely face
So I thought she'd fit right in,
And later, plenty of colour for
My lepidoptera tin.

She flittered and fluttered about the field
While I got my butterfly net,
She'd probably still be fluttering
If I hadn't caught her yet.
But that's how I catch my characters
That I fit in every plot,
I chase them round and I bring them down
Whether they want, or not.

The women are always butterflies,
The men are usually moths,
I struggle to keep the women sweet
But sometimes they are Goths.

As long as they play their part so well
That the reader doesn't twig,
That all my casts are butterflies,
The small parts and the big.

For villains I use the Death's Head Moth
For his markings are so grim,
But the innocent girls in chiffon are
The first to let him in,
He's mean and cunning, and not so sweet
As the ones he seeks to fool,
But I am only the writer, so
Their conflict is my gruel.

I need to go where the sun is bright
And they flutter in the breeze,
To hold my butterfly net upright
And pursue them through the trees.
Then one day soon in the afternoon
I shall write a plot that sings,
And catch me a lepidoptera,
The one with the brightest wings!

Before Trafalgar

I was sat in a Tavern in Pompey Town,
Sipping a tipple of rum,
When I watched a Jack make an axe attack,
Chop off his finger and thumb!

I couldn't believe the blood that flowed
From the cut of that rusty blade,
But the barmaid Flo, said 'You've done it, Joe,
Now look at the mess you've made!'

She cleaned it up with a swill of ale,
Walked off with the finger and thumb,
'I'll nail these up on the balustrade
With the rest that have been as dumb.'

But Joe sang out when he'd had a drink
'It's better than being a tar!
I spent three years, under the lash
On His Majesty's Man o' War.'

'They 'pressed me when I was still a kid
And treated me like a dog,
I suffered scurvy and couldn't work,
The answer to that, was flog.'

'They flogged me around the Southern Cape,
They flogged me a-ship and ashore,
Whenever I thought that I might escape
They dragged me onboard for more.'

'And Cap'n Foggett's abroad tonight
With his cut-throat parcel of rogues,
Impressing the able-bodied men,
They're lining them up in droves.'

'For Nelson's lying abaft the lee
With barely a half a crew,
He needs more men for the 'Victory',
And that means me and you!'

'In every tavern they're moving in,
In every alley and quay,
At first they offer the King's shilling,
To war with the enemy.'

'But the Frenchies rake with the carronade
That will rip the flesh from your bones,
And the decks run red from the men who bled
Impressed from their wives and homes.'

'They say he sails on the tide tonight
So they're doing a quick Hot Press,
Even a gen'lman walking late
Won't meet with their gentleness.'

'A cudgel whack on a squire's head
Then dragged to the bilges, free,
They'll never know 'til they all wake up
That they're headed on out to sea.'

'That Nelson's got but a single arm,
He's got but a single eye,
If that's not enough to be alarmed
By God, then I wonder why!'

The Press Gang came to the Tavern door
But couldn't come on inside,
They tried to sell me a Man o' War
But Joe had made me decide.

I took a gulp of Jamaica Rum
And I steeled myself to the task,
'The Press are waiting outside,' I cried,
'Just hand me that rusty axe!'

If I Thought...

I wanted to go to the end of the street
To buy a chocolate éclair,
But now I'm at the end of the street,
The end of the street's not there.
I'll swear it was there just yesterday,
Was there on the day before,
But now when I look for the end of the street
The end of the street's no more.

All I can see is a land of waste,
A land of rubble and weeds,
Where bushes grow in untidy rows,
A scatter of burdock seeds,
I wander on where the shops have gone
Where you used to meet with us,
But the road just ended around the bend
Where we caught the 16 bus.

There's nothing left but a wilderness
An empty paddock and space,

As if I meet at the end of the street
The end of the human race,
The houses, shops and the industry
And the people I saw before,
They seem to be lost in a history
That nobody felt or saw.

That nobody felt or saw, I thought,
That came and took you away,
Strapped in the back of an ambulance
Laid out on a cold tin tray,
And your laughter fades in the wilderness
And your sighs reach up to the Moon,
And my heart that burst at the back of the hearse
Will never be mended soon.

I wanted to go to the end of the street
To buy a chocolate éclair,
For chocolate's really the only thing
That will feed my deep despair.
But my soul is lost in the wilderness
Of your empty passing by,
I'd spend my grief on the lonely heath
If I thought I could only cry!

The Devil is in the Detail

When Alison left the bath to run
It ruined the parquet floor,
It spilled on out like a waterspout
And ran right under the door,
She'd gone back into the bedroom, so
The spill continued to run,
Across the landing and down the stair,
'Now look what our daughter's done!'

We couldn't dry out the parquetry
It swelled, and loosened the glue,
Then bits would lift and would come adrift,
I didn't know what to do.
Then Barbara said, 'It's coming up,
We shouldn't have laid it down,
I'll go and choose some ceramic tiles
At that tiling place in town.'

I said that I'd lay the tiles myself
But Barbara would insist,
'We really need a professional
For a job as big as this.'
I shrugged, and let her get on with it
I never could win a trick,
So the tiler that she employed was one
Ahab Nathaniel Frick.

I'd seen this tiler about the town
All hunched, and wizened and old,
His wrinkled skin was like parchment in
Some leathery paperfold.

He wore a hat with a drooping brim
So the sun never touched his face,
A puff of wind would have blown him in
To leave not a hint, or trace.

'Are you sure that he's up to this,' I said,
'He isn't the best of men,
He'll probably get on his knees all right
But never get up again.'
But Barbara shushed me out of there
Was keeping me well at bay,
She wanted to prove what she could do
In laying the tiles her way.

I didn't get in to see them then
'Til the tiles were laid, with grout,
Nor see Nathaniel Frick again,
I supposed that he'd gone out.
I stood and stared at the new laid tiles,
Their pattern was in the floor,
And Barbara, waiting proudly said,
'What are you staring for?'

'There's something a-swirl in those tiles,' I said,
'Some pattern you didn't mean,
The way that he's put them together, well
There's a sense of something unclean!'
I said the tiles made an evil face
And showed her the curving jaw,
The squinting eyes that could hypnotise
And the cheeks, so sallow and raw.

She said that she couldn't see it then,
That I must have twisted eyes,

I wasn't wanting to hurt her so
I tried to sympathise,
But the monster's face was set in space
And it wouldn't go away,
I dreamt about that face by night
And I saw it, every day.

At night, the face seemed to snarl at me
When I passed it in the gloom,
And I worried that it was set right there
Outside our daughter's room,
Then Barbara thought she heard a noise,
An intruder in the house,
And tipped me out of the bed to chase
The night intruder out.

The moans began in the early hours
And the groans came just at dawn,
Then Alison came into our room,
'There's a shadow on my wall!
A man with a broad-brimmed, floppy hat
And with squinting eyes that gleamed,'
I said, 'That's it,' when she had a fit
And our darling daughter screamed!

I went on out to the lumber shed
And I brought a mattock in,
While Alison jumped in the double bed
As the tiles set up a din,
A wailing, groaning, squealing sound
That would raise the peaceful dead,
I raised the mattock and smashed the tiles
Just above the monster's head.

The tiles rose up with a mighty roar
And shattered, scattered around,
As a shadow from underneath the floor
Rose up with a dreadful sound,
It hissed, and made for the stairway, leapt
And it almost made me sick,
For fleeing out of the open door
Was Ahab Nathaniel Frick!

The Threat of the Weaker Sex

The man had a terrible temper,
Would rage at the skies above,
Would screech and howl, like a midnight owl,
He'd been unlucky in love.
He'd stomp about in the village square,
Go out, and look for a fight,
The villagers always avoided him
When he'd roam around at night.

Then he'd come and knock at my own front door
Demanding to talk to Jill,
I'd hear her say from the passageway,
'I don't want to talk to Bill!
I'd had enough when he beat me up
And my heart would never heal,
Just tell him I'm sticking with you, my love,
I know that your love is real!'

He'd punch the door, then he'd stand and roar
So I'd slam the door in his face,
He kicked a panel across the floor
And I said I'd call the police!

I heard him muttering as he left,
'Come out, I'll give you a fight,
Tell Jill she's dead if she's in your bed,
I'll call in the dead of night!'

I took the hammer and nails outside
And battened the shutters down,
Then strung an electrical tripwire that
Would pulverise the clown,
'The man's as mad as a meat axe, Jill,
Bi-Polar, that's for sure,'
'More of a schizophrenic, Jim,
'Be sure to bar the door.'

We'd sit in a petrified silence in
The cottage, every night,
Listening for the slightest sound
If something wasn't right,
The roof would creak as the timber cooled
And the wind soughed through the eaves,
We even strained by the window panes
At the patter of Autumn leaves.

'How long are we going to put up with this,'
I said to Jill, one morn,
'He's tempting fate by the garden gate,
He's been there since the dawn.'
'I'm going to have to confront him,' said
The darling of my life,
I hadn't proposed to her just then
But I hoped she'd be my wife.

She walked on out to the garden gate
And I heard him raise his voice,

I couldn't quite make his words out, but
He was giving her a choice.
Then Jill I heard in a voice that stirred
From the depths of a gravel pit,
And he went white with a look of fright
And he left, and that was it!

'What did you say to the maniac
That he turned and went away?'
She smiled, and cuddled on into me,
'I think I made his day.
I said that I'd go back home with him
But I'd poison his meat and drinks,
Or slit his throat when asleep one night…'
He hasn't been back here since!

The Wizard of Did!

I have a man with a pointy hat
Lives under my desktop lid,
He came for muffins and jam, and that,
I call the Wizard of Did,
His beard got caught when the lid came down
So I had to trim it back,
But he says it's comfy and warm in there
So he's turned it into a flat.

I thought at first I would charge him rent
But he wasn't too keen on that,
So I suggested a garden tent
And he said he'd pass the hat.
I'd try to type in the early hours
But he'd bang up under the lid,

'How can I get my beauty sleep,'
He said, the Wizard of Did.

'You're going to have to pay your way,'
I said, 'It's not for free,
'You'd better come up with something good
That's of some use to me.'
'You say you struggle for plots,' he said,
'Well I can help with those,
'I'm full of people I want to be,
I just need different clothes.'

The Wizard was as good as his word
He'd pop up now and then,
Whenever I'd sit and scratch my head
He'd mention Holy men,
Then march along the top of the desk
With mitre, staff and cross,
And make me kiss the pontiff's ring
On the eve of Pentecost.

He'd play the role of a murderer,
He'd play the role of a clown,
He'd play an old sheep herder-er
With a crook in a shepherd's gown,
He'd pop up with a pirate's patch
And tinkle pieces of eight,
Or keep me longing for Molly Brown
When my ship came in too late.

Whenever I sat there at a loss
For a line, a rhyme, a verse,
He'd throw a bag on the table top
And say, 'Now pick a curse!'

He'd turn mine into a haunted house
And he'd stalk me in the gloom,
And have me making a pact with Faust
In a dark and lonely tomb.

And now when I think my muse has gone
That my stories have been spent,
I tap-tap-tap on the table top
And he says, 'You must repent!
I'm not a bottomless pit, you know,'
Climbs in, and closes the lid,
I say, 'You promised a constant flow,'
And he groans, 'I know… I Did!'

Wrong Mountain!

He came on down from the mountain like
An ancient prophet of old,
His hair was long, and fine and white
And his neck was chained with gold,
He carried a staff as he limped on in
To the farm, and asked for a bed,
I said, 'We live in the farmhouse here,
But there's hay in the cattle shed.'

He thanked me then and he stayed the night
I thought he'd be gone at dawn,
But the sun was high on the mountainside
When I saw him stand in the corn,
'Your Lord provides and is bountiful,
You must have kept his commands,
My people wandered for forty years
In the drift of the desert sands.'

I asked him if I could know his name
For the strangers here were few,
He looked askance, but he shook my hand,
'It's Moses, here, to you.
I'm on my way to the Canaanites
Who possess my promised lands,
But I need to know where I have to go
I'm a stranger in your hands.'

I thought he must have been wandering,
Some defect of the mind,
I said, 'You're not on the continent
That you want so hard to find,
That mountain there isn't Sinai,
We're far too south to gauge,
This farm's in Eastern Australia
By the Great Dividing Range.

He shook his head and his eyes went dead
And he turned towards the creek,
It was riding high with a swollen tide
For the best part of a week,
I thought, he'll never get over that,
The current is far too strong,
But he beat his staff on the bank, three times,
How could I be so wrong?

The water parted, it ceased to flow,
But it raised in two tall towers,
Then he set off in the midst of it,
I sat in shock for hours,
The last I saw he was marching off
As the creek collapsed to flow,
I thought, 'and the best of British luck,
You've a helluva way to go!'

Only the View

I like to walk on the beach, I said,
As it sweeps around in the bay,
There isn't a single building here
To rise, or get in the way,
It's as it was when the world was formed
For only the tides will change,
And God sits there in his easy chair,
There's nothing to rearrange.

You brought me here when the sky was clear
In the first full flush of love,
Your eyes met mine, they were so divine
And I thanked the Lord above,
For what were the chances of meeting you
In the larger scale of things,
Angels are usually out of view
But they gave your soul bright wings.

It was just by chance, but I saw you dance
When you thought you were on your own,
But I was out in the park at dawn
When you fluttered down from your throne,
I thought my eyes had been mesmerised
When you twisted, turned and spun,
That perfect grace, and an angel's face
In the rays of the morning sun.

You brought me here to this lonely beach
Where the love we made was fun,
But then you said it was out of reach
It would soon be dead and gone,

For nothing as fine as this could last
It was tempting fate, you said,
And 'darker shadows will come to pass'
Were the words I came to dread.

The season is brief for everything
For life, you said, for love,
And youth is merely the briefest dream
When it comes to push and shove,
But I walk the beach now the years have gone
With the memories that we share,
But now you share them from up above
With God asleep in his chair.

The future yawns, for we're just the pawns
In some sad, celestial game,
A brief exposure to happiness
And the rest in eternal pain,
So I walk the beach for I try to reach
The days I was here with you,
Your shadow teases me at the breach,
In the end, there's only the view.

Bell, Book & Candle

The Church in its awesome majesty
Looked down, from over the hill,
From faith, to hope, to travesty
It stood, and is standing still,
So proud in its fine regalia
Its ritual, and never the least,
Its potent God who would wield his rod
Deter the jaws of the beast.

The Bishop of Saint Ignatius Church
Was a proud and holy man,
Who wouldn't suffer the jibes of fools
From Rome to Afghanistan,
And certainly not those down the hill
In the new Masonic Lodge,
That beastly, secret doctrine that
He advised his flock to dodge.

He'd stand at the steps of his church and stare
Down at the barbarians,
He hated Lodges, he hated Mosques
And Rastafarians,
'There shouldn't be anyone else but me,
I hold the eternal God,
What gods they worship could never be,
For they're all distinctly odd.'

While down at the Lodge of the Masons
They were cool with their golden rule,
They had to believe in a god as such,
But how, it was up to you.

For some would practice the Baptist faith,
And some Presbyterian,
While some enrolled in the Primitive state
Were a type of Wesleyan.

There was only a single Catholic
And he wore a glued on rug,
He wanted to still be young at heart,
Was known as the Grand HumBug,
The Antidiluvian Mason's Guild
Was the name he'd chosen himself,
The others differed, but he was keen,
And he was the one with wealth.

Their God was known as the Architect,
They carried the masons tools,
The set square set them apart from all
The disbelievers and fools.
They worked on their secret rituals
And kept a goat at the back,
For leading a blindfold novice in
And guarding the Lodge from attack.

The Bishop heard that a Catholic
Was leading the Masons there,
He fumed, choked on his rhetoric, but
Was heard to firmly declare,
'I will not shelter a wayward sheep
Who has taken to ways I hate,
The only fate for a traitor here
Is to excommunicate!'

He gathered a dozen priests to march
With candles, down to the Hall,

Surrounded the base heretic's Lodge
And named HumBug in his call,
Sprinkled his holy water 'til
It fizzed, and gave off a smell,
Doused his candle and closed his book,
Consigning the man to Hell!

But Humbug patted his glued on rug
Went out, untethered the goat,
He let it loose on the dozen Priests,
It butted the Bishop's coat,
They ran in confusion up the street,
To the church, set up on the hill,
While the goat was hard at the Bishop's heels
Like a demon released from Hell.

It butted the Bishop's altar and
It charged, knocked over the font,
Scattered the pews for the devil's dues
In a hellfire sacrament,
While HumBug muttered he might end up
In Hell, with his Mason's sect,
But the Bishop's God, had failed with his rod
In a clash with his Architect!

The Shadow Makers

I recall I lay at the top of the hill
A toboggan, all set to go,
My friend behind, and urging me on
We'd had a good fall of snow,
I was lying flat, head first on that
When we hurtled on down the hill,
My friend was dragging his feet to steer,
He steered to a certain spill.

A clump of trees in the valley below,
I told him to steer out wide,
But he dragged his foot with his hob-nailed boot,
I knew we were going to collide,
The tree came up like a railway train
There were stars and I lay there still
A piece of branch was lodged in my brain
From the tree at the base of the hill.

They said I'd never survive, I know,
They said I'd surely be dead,
With a length of fir tree, covered in blood
And sticking right out of my head.
I was out of it for a month or more,
A coma of long lost time,
But finally woke in the hospital
To find I was almost blind.

All I could see were shadows, shades
That drifted in silent space,
These shadows all were as black as coal
And none of them had a face,

As if I was seeing a different world
To the one I'd always been in,
And one of them sidled on up to me,
'You're seeing the world of sin!'

I couldn't see when the nurses came
But I heard them when they spoke,
A doctor came, said 'it's such a shame,
So sad for the little bloke!'
Three shadows were hanging on every word
As they lounged near the further wall,
And then I knew that they stuck like glue
For the Doc had done for them all!

They sent me home to recuperate
Sat out in an easy chair,
The garden looked like a negative
Of a black and white picture there,
My parents slowly came into view
But the shades stood out by the fence,
I'd always thought they were both sin free
But their sins were there, past tense.

My friend from the great toboggan spill
Came to visit me there to see
If I'd suspect that he'd steered direct,
Deliberately into the tree,
But a shadow hung at his shoulder there
And it gave his game away,
The shadow was mine, and over time
Will be there 'til his dying day.

We're all of us shadow makers when
We're sinned against, done wrong,

We don't have to be earth shakers, but
That sin will never be gone.
My sight has slowly recovered now
But I wonder, now I am back,
How many shadows are following me,
And when are they going to attack?

Crimson Dawn

There's an angel down in my garden plot
But she's overgrown with weeds,
She looms up out of the sassafras
Set back in among the trees.
I don't know how long she's stood out there
But her wings are green with moss,
And her tired face is a study in grace,
Reflecting a sense of loss.

'Your flesh was an alabaster white
But it's almost faded to grey,
You're weather-worn, and you look forlorn
As if you've been cast away.
The days when you were a centrepiece
Of a garden, laid and fine,
Have now passed on, with the garden gone
But I've found you now, you're mine.'

'I promise I'll clear the weeds away,
I'll scrub the moss from your wings,
I'll light that tender smile on your face
With the glow a spotlight brings,
I'll bring you back to the glory you
Reflect from heaven's spell,

And people will come adoring you
When I put in a wishing well.'

'A wishing well for your hopes and dreams
And the hopes and dreams of them,
They'll touch your gown and they'll toss a coin
When they leave, they'll wish you well.
I'll sleep with you looking over me
And dream of the King of Kings,
And see his crown as he's looking down
We'll see what the future brings!'

I worked to see my promises kept
'Til the angel gleamed and shone,
But one day there in the garden wept
For the angel there had gone.
She'd fluttered off from her plinth one night
With her feathered wings reborn,
And through my tears, and despite my fears
I rejoiced at the Crimson Dawn!

Bad Christmas!

I've had a terrible day today
The horse had broken a shoe,
I had to get to the marketplace
And didn't know what to do,
So I borrowed the neighbour's horse and cart
Was stopped by the local cop,
He said that the stuff on the neighbour's cart
Had been stolen, from a shop!

He wouldn't believe it wasn't mine
And locked me up in a cell,
I'm being done for the stolen goods
And the stolen cart as well.
It took them hours to bail me out
Then I had to walk back home,
Fifteen miles to the mountain top
And the tongue of a rabid crone.

'Why do you always do these things,
Why is it always you?
The guy next door, he never gets caught
But he's so much smarter - True!'
I didn't think she'd ever give up,
My dinner was down the drain,
They say that marriage is so much bliss,
Then why is there so much pain?

The kids were screaming about the place
When they should have been in bed,
She said she couldn't control them, but
At least the kids were fed.

I bit a crust that was far too old
And it almost broke my teeth
Then saw the thing was covered in mould,
All that I want is Sleep!

'All that I want is sleep,' I said
As I staggered off to my room,
It seemed a conspiracy overhead
Was acting out in the gloom,
A crash, a clash on the tiles above
I thought it was drunken Joe,
He's always fooling about at night,
Him and his 'Ho ho ho!'

The wife snuck into the bedroom then
And she said, 'Don't make a peep!
Or Father Christmas will hear you, Ben,
You ought to be sound asleep!'
My eyes bugged out and I leapt on up
Flung open the window wide,
'And how do you think I'm supposed to sleep
With you pissing about outside!'

I heard the chomping of many teeth
And a very distinctive 'Neigh!'
Stuck my head out so far that I
Could see this silver sleigh.
I yelled, 'Hey get off my effing roof,
You're damaging all my tiles!'
And then this guy in a bright red suit
Looked down, his face all smiles.

All he could say was 'Ho ho ho',
He'd come from some funny farm,

I yelled, 'Do you want a bunch of fives?'
He started to look alarmed.
I heard the rattle of antler horns
As he started to ride away,
I couldn't believe my eyes to see
It was Santa's Silver Sleigh!

They've stuck me out in the doghouse here,
I had to kick out the dog,
But found, at least, that his rug was fleece
I could sleep at last, like a log.
There'd better not be another day
Like this, as I said to Steve,
'You'd think that someone would warn me when
It's coming up Christmas Eve!'

The Guilt Trip

The storm outside was abating, or
He thought that it was, at first,
He'd only gone to the pub with Joe
To slake a raging thirst.
They'd both been out on the landfill
And it was humid through the day,
So Joe said, 'Bet I can race you there
And put two pints away!'

But the storm had built as they drank in there
And the rain came down in sheets,
Then hailstones peppered the windows and
Joe said, 'It's turned to sleet!
I think we're not going anywhere
'Til the storm has passed and gone,

We might as well have another..
And it's your shout,' he said to John.

They'd known each other forever, and
Had married two sisters, late,
They'd both been into their thirties,
Sister Jean and sister Kate.
While one of them was a loving match,
The other one was mean,
And Joe said, 'would you consider a swap,
My Kate for her sister, Jean?'

So John had laughed, but he looked away
For he knew that Joe was sore,
For Kate was never the bargain that
His mate was looking for,
Her tongue was sharp, though he knew her bark
Was worse that her fabled bite,
For John was meeting Kate in the dark
When they both were alone at night.

He'd kick himself, for he knew that Jean
Was the love match of the pair,
But she tended to work at night so much
That she often wasn't there,
And Joe would stay at the pub so late
That they had to throw him out,
He didn't have cause to go back home
So he stayed until last shout.

The storm continued to rage outside
So they both got worse for drink,
And the talk died down as they sat and frowned,
They both had time to think.

'We're always going to be mates,' said John,
'I hope that you think so too.'
'We're side by side where we both belong
No matter what we might do.'

But the booze brought on a maudlin state
And it seemed to get to John,
'It may be time to confess,' he thought,
'This deception can't go on.
I've something I have to tell you, Joe,
It's time I was coming clean.'
But Joe stayed him, and he said, 'Me first!
Old mate, I've been seeing Jean!'

What Happens?

What happens to love that's neglected,
What happens with absence of care,
When only the shrug of indifference
Is left for you both to share.
What happens when neither will reach on out
To touch, or caress or to hold,
Or eyes never meet when you pass in the street
There's a shrivelling up of the soul.

And the taste of the past is like ashes,
While the memories gone are like dust,
Growing deeper with time as it passes
To bury attraction and lust.
And you wonder about the excitement
That you felt at the moment you met,
Was that a mirage, is the desert so large
That your heart remains lost in it yet?

When the days stretch ahead, and are endless
That you fear there will be no respite,
Are you under a curse, could it be any worse
With your tears on the pillow at night?
When you put a brave face on each morning,
And you nod to each other, then go,
But pray life will not be extended,
What happens? I think that you know!

Nadine

Nadine was naïve when she came to me,
So innocent, fresh and sublime,
I found that I had to pinch myself
When she told me she was mine.
She was barely out of her teens back then
While I was over the hill,
She hadn't a toe in the water then,
But I had been through the mill.

Her gentle face was a study in grace
And her eyes had sparkled blue,
Her hair like a field of waving corn
And her lips had glistened dew,
Her breasts were fresh, pushed under her dress
And her hips a promised world,
I'd watch her sway as she'd drift my way
This seductive, sensuous girl.

I'd lie on the bed after making love
And I'd watch her rise and move,

She'd pose for me in her poetry
Like a picture, hung in the Louvre.
She was never ashamed of her body then
Though she lent it just to me,
The rest of the world was missing out,
It was pure idolatry.

I'd take her walking to see the sites
Where culture lurked in the gloom,
And art then captured her simple heart
As we'd go from room to room,
Rubens, Degas and Cabanel,
Titian, Goya, Courbet,
She said, 'I want to be seen like that,
Preserved in a youthful way.'

We met the sculptor, Matthias Krohn
At a gallery in Berlin,
His mouth fell open to see Nadine
With her pale and perfect skin.
'You have a goddess, my friend,' he said,
'I must capture her in stone!'
I said, 'Can I come along and watch?'
'I must work with her alone.'

I'd drop Nadine at his studio
Each day, and she'd stay 'til four,
I'd ask her how it was going, and
She'd shrug, wouldn't tell me more.
'The sculpture's facing away from me
I won't see it 'til it's done.'
I could tell by the downcast look of her
That it wasn't really fun.

'It's cold, it gets very cold in there,'
She said, when a month had gone
And that was the first time that I knew
She was posed, no clothing on.
'I thought he would drape your figure there,
In something filmy, like lawn,
'I told him I wanted the world to see me
Naked as I was born.'

The months went on, there was something wrong
The sparkle had gone from her eye,
The hair that had been like waving corn
Was now just brittle and dry,
Her lips were pursed in a moody line,
No longer glistened with dew,
I said, 'Am I doing something wrong…'
'It's nothing to do with you!'

I went on the final day with her,
Matthias ushered us in,
'You've come for my greatest masterpiece,'
But all I could see was sin.
The eyes were cynical, looking down,
The lips were curled in contempt,
The breasts were pert like a blatant flirt
Who basked in her element.

I took one look at the parted legs
And reached for my girl, Nadine,
The tears were streaming along her cheeks,
'You've made me appear unclean!'
Matthias shrugged as she rushed on out,
'It's true to the girl I saw.'
'Your evil eyes must have told you lies,
You've turned Nadine to a whore!'

She never came back to our home again,
She wandered the streets in shame,
I tried to find her, to track her down
But I heard she was on the game.
I saw her last, get into a car,
Her lips were curled in contempt,
Her hair was brittle, like faded straw
But she looked in her element!

The Tale on a Bloodied Screed

We were swept up onto this rocky coast
By a storm in '93,
There were thirteen passengers and crew
And a stowaway, that's me!
The ship was holed on the jagged rocks
And it sits still out in the bay,
We've never been able to fix the hole
So it looks like here we'll stay.

It sits forlorn when the tide is low
But is covered when it's high,
As the breakers beat on the after decks
Though the ship is never dry.
The water pours from the cabins, and
Lies deep in the forward hold,
While the rust is eating the hull away
And the cargo's turned to mould.

We thought that we'd soon be rescued
By a ship just passing by,

But all we saw for a month or more
Was the lonely sea and the sky,
We made our camp on the beach where we
Could watch for a passing light,
And cook our fish on the signal fires,
But the trouble came at night.

The crew of seven were restless and
The passengers were few,
For only five of us men were there
And the women, only two.
One, the wife of a clergyman
The other a girl called Gail,
And she was sweet on a man called Deet
That she'd met before we sailed.

But Deet had fought with the bosun
Over the fish he said were his,
They moved away, went around the bay
To seek their Island bliss.
That left the clergyman's wife with us
Who was praying we'd be found,
But late one night, in another fight
The clergyman was drowned.

The bosun dragged her away from us
With Froggat, Jones and Lees,
They took the struggling woman with them
Deep into the trees,
There wasn't a thing we could do for her
So we went out to the ship,
And armed ourselves with iron bars
While we told ourselves: 'They'll keep!'

We moved our camp from the other crew
For the feeling there was mean,
The three the bosun had left behind
Hid out where they'd not be seen,
But then, at just about midnight we
Were hearing an eerie wail,
For down at the beach they'd murdered Deet
And dragged off the weeping Gail.

From deep in the trees we saw that Lees
Was trying to reach our spot,
His head was covered in blood, but then
He fell from a single shot,
The bosun was dragging Marie, the wife
To the open, by her hair,
Her dress was soiled and her face was spoiled
With the tears of a deep despair.

We didn't see Froggat and Jones again,
They'd fallen to the knife,
But I had to run from the bosun's gun
In order to stay alive,
Then under the cover of darkness we
Went after the weeping Gail,
And beneath the stars with our iron bars
We left a bloodied trail.

We caught the bosun asleep one night
And we beat him with our bars,
He didn't have time to wake before
We dispatched him to the stars,
That left just Jeremy Leach and I
And the women that we'd saved,
For Gordon died of a fever then
And we dug his sandy grave.

It looks as if we'll be here for good
So I'll sign this bloodied screed,
Place it safe in a bottle then
And commit it to the seas,
We won't fight over the women for
Marie is now with Leach,
And Gail has a tiny stowaway
As she wanders along the beach.

Two Paths...

The path that I like to wander on
Is a rural lane in the trees,
It's a pleasant walk, and I tend to talk
To myself, just shooting the breeze.
Then it comes to a wood, and it parts in two
The main path tends to the right,
And heads up 'til, just over the hill
It's bathed in a pure sunlight.

And there stands a mansion in plain stucco
With columns that hold up a porch,
And each of the windows send out a beam
As of someone, holding a torch,
A woman dressed plainly in white comes out,
Invites me to come in for tea,
Then sometimes I do, and sometimes I don't,
But we spend our time pleasantly.

We sit in a kitchen that's tiled in white
And the sunlight beams through the door,
She sometimes reads to me from a book,

And asks what I'm looking for.
I tell her I'm totally lost, and then
Confusion's writ over my face,
So she makes the sign of the saviour's cross,
And blesses me with her grace.

The other path veers off to the left,
Is narrow and mean through the trees,
It slopes on down to a valley with grass
Though a turn in the path deceives.
For hidden there in the undergrowth
Is a cottage in shadow, and grim,
Where a gypsy girl with an evil smile
Beckons for me to come in.

And sometimes I do, and sometimes I don't,
She isn't offering tea,
She dances and whirls in the kitchen there,
And sometimes, sits on my knee.
She places my hand on her silken thigh,
And asks what I'm looking for,
I tell her I'm totally lost, and then
I struggle on out of her door.

A poet once said that he took the path,
The one less travelled by,
I've tried them both, and I still go back
To the ones both low, and high.
For my soul is soothed by the woman in white,
She lifts me up to the heights,
But the gypsy girl puts my mind in a whirl
And she sates my darker nights.

Dead Man's Eyes

He was hanging in line with the elder trees
From an oak that had broken the line,
That's why they probably missed him, he
Became as one in design.
He wore a shabby old overcoat
But his hat lay there on the ground,
It wasn't until a jogger who fell
Looked up, that the man was found.

The firemen cut his body down
While the police stood back a pace,
Then loaded him into an ambulance
With a consequent lack of grace.
His eyes were staring, his jaw was slack
And his arms flopped north and south,
But most of all, and what appalled
Was the purple tongue in his mouth.

Nobody seemed to know who he was
His clothing tags had been cut,
There wasn't a wallet or envelope
In the pockets of his old coat.
'He must be someone, but who knows who?
And why was he hanging there?
Could this have been murder or suicide,
And really, does anyone care?'

He didn't come up on the Missing List,
Nor his face on a Mug Shot file,
No-one was desperately phoning in,
He must have been gone for a while.

'There's a picture there, on his retina,'
The photographer said at last,
'If we blow it up, it might give us a clue,
What he saw at his final gasp.'

The rope had been knotted behind his neck
So his head had been angled down,
His eyes had bulged as the blood withdrew
And snapped what he saw on the ground.
A woman was stood there, looking up
With an anguished look on her face,
Her hands together, as if in prayer
But holding a can of Mace.

The police supplied an identikit
And published it over the news,
They passed it around the prison guards
And questioned most of the Screws.
But they didn't mention the woman there
Reflected in each of his eyes,
They kept that piece of forensic back
As their own well kept surprise.

The plain clothes men at the funeral
Were alert, but hid in the trees,
They'd made it known where the man was going
And when, to the cemetery,
So when a woman in black appeared
To watch as the coffin fell,
They swooped, and took her in charge right then
As she cried, 'I've been in Hell!'

She cried all over the interview,
They thought that her heart would break,

'I messed right up,' was her one refrain,
'It was one great big mistake!
We'd been together, over a year
And I loved him, he was nice,
But then he began to dabble in drugs
And he played about with ice.'

'I begged and begged, but he wouldn't stop,
And his violent side came out,
He ran amok and he wrecked our home
And he'd start to scream and shout,
I should have gone to the police right then,
Should have had him in rehab,
But I bought the Mace to protect myself,
I know, you must think I'm mad!'

'Then he'd sober up, see what he'd done
And would be so full of remorse,
I had to forgive him, every time
Just as a matter of course,
Until the day that he knocked me down
And I said, 'No going back!
I can't put up with this any more,'
Then he took the rope from the shack.'

'I followed him into the woods out there
And I tried to talk him down,
But he climbed the oak and he tied the rope
And he told me, with a frown,
'The devil has got me by the throat
And I died when hitting you,
I'll never deserve of your love again
What a terrible thing to do!'

'Then he jumped,' she said, and burst the dam
For her tears would never stop,
She went back into the woods again
To plant forget-me-nots,
And I heard she'd died of a broken heart
And was buried where he lies,
But still lives on in that photograph
As seen in a dead man's eyes!

The Call of the Sea

He wandered along the decks by night,
Stood at the rails by day,
Kept to himself from what I saw
And didn't have much to say,
He wore a yellow sou'wester when
The weather came in cold,
And a battered and worn old Navy cap
With the legend 'Merchant Gold'.

He must have been once a seaman
In a time quite long ago,
He still had his steady seaman's legs
On the 'Michaelangelo',
A crusty and time-worn cruise ship
That had seen much better days,
Pottering round the islands through
The softly lapping waves.

I doubt that it could withstand a storm
It was just a summer cruise,
For a raggedy band of tourists who
Had nothing much to lose,

The fares were cheap and the cabins bare
So I utilised the bar,
While the wife would wander off and say,
'I'll know just where you are!'

I got in some serious drinking
There was nothing else to do,
While Helen came back with every name
Of the stewards, and the crew,
For Helen's a social butterfly
And she loves to gad about,
I've never been much of a talker
So I tend to shut her out.

One night I happened to wander out
She was over by the rail,
Listening to the sailor who
Was reading her some tale,
I turned back into the dining room
Until my wife was free,
Then asked her: 'What was he reading?'
And she said, 'Some poetry!'

'A poem called 'Sea Fever' that had
Brought a tear to his eye,
It was all about a tall ship
And a star to steer her by,
If only you could have heard him, Ben
He had such a tale to tell,
I could have listened to him for hours,
His soul is like a well.'

'His life was spent on the water and
He calls it God's domain,

He said that having to leave it brought
His life's most constant pain,
He pointed the constellations out
Named every little star,
He gave me a feeling of awe about
The ocean, where we are.'

I know I must have been jealous for
I never took the bait,
I didn't talk to the sailor,
When I would, it was too late,
A storm blew up and the rising seas
Crashed over the decks and spars,
While he clung onto the outer rails
And gazed on up at the stars.

And then I must have been seeing things
For a man approached him there,
Holding onto a trident with
Coiled seaweed in his hair,
Touched him once with the trident and
The sailor turned his head,
Nodded once, with a gentle smile
Then draped on the rail, was dead.

They gathered the poor old sailor up
And bound him up in a sheet,
Waited until the sea calmed down
Called everyone to meet,
Then after a simple service they
Just slipped him into the sea,
A fitting end for a sailor who
Had left our company.

But Helen was broken hearted she
Was weeping all day long,
While I was irritated, and
I asked her, what was wrong?
She stopped and smiled, and she said, 'Oh well,
He's back in the sea he loved,
In a tall ship with a broad sail,
With the sky and the stars above!'

I think of him, and Neptune with
A trident, on his throne,
The sailor reading poetry
But this time, quite alone,
While coral reefs and gentle seas
Pay tribute to his life,
But I couldn't share it now with him…
He shared it with my wife!

('Sea Fever' by John Masefield)

The Wages of Sin...

The Lady Mary had locked the door
And called the scullery maid,
The Boots was called and the Footman,
So they thought they were being paid,
She lined them up with the Butler,
The Housemaid, skivvy and Cook,
'You're not to go wandering out the door,
Not even to take a look!'

She knew her word, though the very law,
Was never to go down well,
For Alice was sweet on a lawyer's clerk,
A lockdown seemed like hell.
The Footman needed his racing mates
To place a bet on the book,
So the Lady Mary had made it plain,
'Not even a peep or a look!'

The grumbling went with the Cook downstairs
As they stood, and waited for tea,
'It's all very well for the likes of her,
There's places I have to be!'
'Enough of this nonsense,' the Butler said,
'We're lucky to grace her floor,
If you want to leave in a fit of peeve
You'll never get back in the door.'

They huddled down for a week or more
It was better than paying rent,
But a silence settled on every floor
For nobody came, or went,

The pantry shelves were emptying out
But the tradesmen never came,
'We're going to starve,' was the one lament
When they ate the last of the game.

The Footman called the Scullery Maid
And they huddled up on a pew,
'If you sneak out for an hour tonight,
Then I will cover for you,
And you can visit your lawyer's clerk
Then place a bet on the book,
I'll let you in when it's nice and dark…'
'I will, by hook or by crook!'

She slipped on out by the kitchen door
And he turned the key in the lock,
Watched the Butler heading for bed
And sat by the kitchen clock.
At ten o'clock, with a tiny tap
She had made her prescence felt,
And tumbled in as he opened the door,
Went straight to the hearth, and knelt.

He locked the door, then he heard her sob
And saw that her head was bent,
She stared so long and hard at the floor
That he thought his bet was spent.
'What ails you Alice, now what went wrong,
Don't give me none of your lies!'
She looked up into his face just then
And he saw blood stream from her eyes!'

'They're dead, all dead,' were the words she said
As her tears had mixed with the blood,

Your racing pals and my lawyers clerk,
And the horses, down at the stud.
The Lady Mary, she should have said…'
But he cut her off right there,
Leapt up, unlocking the kitchen door
He dragged her out by her hair.

He locked the door and he scrubbed his hands
But he'd locked the beast within,
As blood then streamed from his Footman's eyes
And he earned the wages of sin.
The Lady Mary came down the stair
To find him, dead on the floor,
And said to the Cook, with blood red eyes,
'You'd best fling open the door!'

Auto-da-fé

The three of us had been travelling
For weeks, and were getting tired,
We'd taken pictures of everything
And our visas had expired,
We got a room in a gloomy house
And we settled down to wait,
For Julie wanted to sleep a lot
While Francis stood at the gate.

For he was the moody, restless one,
And wanted to travel back,
I was just glad to settle down
And dump my heavy pack,
I took a seat at the window ledge
And I read a magazine,

While Julie said that the light was bad,
'You'll ruin your vision, Dean!'

It certainly was a gloomy room
And the walls were painted brown,
We'd had to look for the cheapest in
An ancient part of town,
The concierge was a Capuchin
With a tonsure and a cross,
I felt like I had to bow to him
As he passed the keys across.

The room had merely a single bulb
That would only work at night,
And then, it had such a feeble beam
You could hardly call it bright,
But when it lit we could see at last
On the further, darkest wall,
There hung a dusty old painting that
We hadn't seen before.

It blended in with the wall behind
For the tones were shades of brown,
The face of an old Franciscan who
Was looking sadly down,
But in his eyes was a faint surprise
As of one with mystic deeps,
And Francis said that it turned his head,
'Those eyes give me the creeps!'

We ate a couple of sandwiches
And we turned in for the night,
We didn't think it was worth it but
We still turned out the light,

Then I awoke in the early hours
To the sound of cries and shrieks,
The volume gradually rising
As my skin began to creep.

A sudden flare lit the room in there
From the painting on the wall,
The crackling sound of flames devouring
The monk, I was appalled,
And through the flames I could see those eyes
As they bored into the room,
And then, the crackling disappeared
And the room was plunged in gloom.

There wasn't a sign of damage to
The painting, or the wall,
But a whisp of sulphur and brimstone
Hung in the air, and overall,
While Francis huddled in terror with
His face as pale as sleet,
And Julie couldn't stop sobbing then
From underneath her sheet.

We snatched our stuff in the morning
And I handed back the keys,
I said, 'Just who is that picture of?'
The concierge looked pleased.
'That's just one of the Franciscans
Who rebelled against the Pope,
He went to the Inquisition then
And they gave him little hope.'

'Four of the monks were burned out there
As a lesson to the rest,

St. Francis would have approved, they were
Schismatic, at the best,
This is the town the Inquisition
Righted many a wrong,
They burned the recusant catholics
In the square at Avignon.'

Francis had left before us, he
Refused to wait in there,
He wandered out with his backpack and
Stood waiting in the square,
Just as the petrol tanker rolled,
From a worn and faulty tyre,
And the last I saw, he was standing there
Engulfed in a lake of fire!

Hadron Hell!

Is it God out there in the woods tonight
Or some weird, unhallowed troll,
Uprooting trees in the scorching breeze
With a dread that shreds my soul,
The sky is glowering red like blood
For a warning, in advance,
Since ever the Hadron Collider fired
And swallowed half of France.

A planet, black as a pit of tar
Has appeared just up on high,
Has popped up out of some x-ray realm
And filled up half the sky,
The earth is teetering on the edge
Of a black hole, forged in space,

And threatening us with extinction,
What's left of the human race.

It was all for the sake of science, so
They told us, overall,
To add to their fount of knowledge like
The new God Particle,
Though why they wanted to raise it when
There is no recompense,
As it ravages half of the planet,
What did they use for common sense?

There's a hole down deep in the ocean that
Is swallowing half the sea,
The earth it quakes, and volcanoes
Are erupting frequently,
While we lie low in our cottage home
To the growling in the woods,
From some atavistic animal
Unwrapped from its hellish shrouds.

The ones who unleashed this savage beast
Have all been swallowed whole,
Are floating in some dimension in
Their Hadron hidey-hole,
We should have had them arrested long
Before they hatched their plot,
Lined them up with their arrogance,
Their science, and had them shot!

Photographs

His parents had both been gone so long
He'd forgotten how they looked,
So gathered up all the photographs
And pasted them in a book,
Then hid the book until once a year
He would bring it out in the light,
And ruffle through all of its pages in
A memorial delight.

His wife said, 'Why do you bother, Ken,
It will never bring them back,
It's surely enough to remember when
You left, on a different track.'
Her own had consciously turned away
When she went and married Ken,
Had spurned her later advances and
She hadn't seen them again.

'I gave my family up for you,
But what did you do for me?
You tied me down with your family plan,
Locked me in your family tree!'
'Was that so bad?' And he looked quite sad
She revealed what he'd always known,
That she'd always hated his parents and
Would rather they'd lived alone.

'What did they ever do to you,' he said
'To warrant your gall?'
'They took away from my time with you,
With them, they wanted it all.'

'They simply wanted the best for us
So they helped us out where they could.'
'They kept on coming around,' she said,
'A great deal more than they should!'

One year, on opening up his book
There was more than a missing page,
With some of the photo's gone for good
He was flung in a sullen rage.
'What have you done with the photographs
Of the folks, there, back on the farm?'
'You must have mislaid the things yourself…'
And he looked at her in alarm.

'Have you gone really quite mad,' he said,
'Have you gone really insane?
Why would you take my memories
And cause me so much pain?'
'They're gone, they're dead,' she had screamed at him,
'Yet you never let them be,
As long as you still remember them,
Then I will never be free!'

'I thought that I'd seen the last of them
When I put your mother away,
And then, with only your father left
I made sure he choked that day!
I needed to get a new life for me
I need to be more than a wife…'
She hurriedly poured his soup for him
As he slowly picked up the knife.

The Phantom Bus

She didn't look awfully well that day
Though she never would make a fuss,
I said we should get to the hospital
That I'd travel with her on the bus.
The weather was terrible, snow on the road
And a seaborne yellow mist,
So I wrapped her well in a scarf and coat
And did my best to assist.

She leant on me, walked out to the stop
And we sat on the ice cold bench,
I thought for a moment she'd faint or drop
So taking the bus made sense.
The car would be hard to manage that night
For the roads were covered with ice,
I couldn't hold her while driving the car,
But we needed a doctor's advice.

The cough had got worse as the day went on
And her hanky was spattered with blood,
I prayed it was just a vessel that burst,
Not that I thought it should,
But consumption sat at the back of my mind
It was rare, but still around,
I was praying a lot, but still my head
Would cover the same old ground.

We watched as the lights of the bus rolled up
So dim in the mist to see,
A double-decker, we climbed aboard
It was number twenty-three.

The passengers all were grey and drab
And some of them seemed asleep,
A skeleton sat hunched up at the rear
And Kathie began to weep.

'It's only a medical student's thing,'
I said, 'there's nothing to fear.'
But Kathie flinched as we walked on past,
'Then why did he leave it here?'
She settled down in a window seat
While I sat next to the aisle,
And the bus rolled into the swirling mist
So we sat quite still for a while.

The lights in the bus were more than dim
And Kathie was looking grey,
While I got up at the hospital stop
Kathie was looking away.
Then suddenly I was out on the road
As the bus took off in the mist,
While Kathie stared through the window pane,
It was like she didn't exist.

I ran and I ran, and chased the bus,
But I ran and ran in vain,
For the bus veered off, went over the cliffs
And vanished into the rain,
I found her there on the bus stop bench
Where we'd sat, all grey and still,
And I wept, and thought of the phantom bus
That had taken her over the hill.

I could swear we'd stood, and climbed on the bus,
My love, my Kathie and me,

But they said there never was such a bus
As a number twenty-three,
And I see her now in my dreams at night
As she stares through the window pane,
Of a phantom bus that takes her away,
Over the cliffs in the rain.

Over the cliffs on a freezing night
When she died, ice cold on the bench,
What was I thinking, I ask myself,
Where was my common sense?
Then I take some comfort to think that I
Had once been a part of us,
And travelled some of the way with her
Where she'd gone, on the phantom bus.

Powerless!

The sun had not even risen when
Delaney opened his eyes,
To colours, bent through a prism, and
Rotating there in the skies.
He thought it might be the Northern Lights
But they're not seen that far south,
And with them came a crackling sound
To sow the first seeds of doubt.

He rose and walked to the window,
To stand by the sliding door
That led to his private balcony
On the hundred and twentieth floor,
The world below was in darkness and
In shock, he began to shout:

'Hey Mary, get up and look at this,
The lights of the city are out!'

The lights of the city were out, all right,
There wasn't a glimmer of light,
In all the teeming metropolis
Not even a car's headlight.
Mary sleepily rose from bed
And joined him there by the door,
'It isn't the dark that does my head,
What's that on the balcony floor?'

And there in the shade of the balcony
Was standing a monstrous beast,
Its talons several inches long,
Its beak was a foot, at least,
It suddenly opened enormous wings
Then steadily folded them back,
With eyes that promised a thousand things
And one, the threat of attack.

It saw them there through the plated glass
And rushed across for its prey,
Hit the glass and it looked surprised
The two were backing away.
'Call the firemen, call the police,
That thing will need to be shot.'
'The signal seems to have gone astray,
And the cell phone's all we've got!'

The sun came up through the morning mist
And it lit the city square,
Delaney got his binoculars,
Nothing was moving there.

The power was out, so there was no doubt
They were locked in their flat, for sure,
The door to the stairwell wouldn't budge
On the hundred and twentieth floor.

No light, no heat, and down in the street
No cars that streamed that day,
It was just as if electricity
Had suddenly gone away.
Their door had a pin, and powered lock
As did every door below,
A hundred and twenty floors locked in
With nowhere they could go.

The day wore on in the morning sun
And the birds had multiplied,
Looking like pterodactyls they
Swooped over the countryside,
And five came down on the balcony
Of Delaney and Mary's flat,
The food in the fridge was spoiling as
The ice dripped out on the mat.

They couldn't cook, they couldn't eat,
They couldn't open a can,
The electric opener wouldn't work
Nor the cleverer works of man,
And the pterodactyls sat in a row
Out on the balcony floor,
With eyes of hate they would sit and wait
Til someone slid open the door!

Threatening Rain

It was threatening rain for a week or more
It was always threatening rain,
The Weather Bureau was always sore
When the threatening rain never came.
We'd hold an open air barbecue
Each time they said it would come,
'Hey it's gonna rain,' said Oliver Payne,
'What do they think, we're dumb?'

But the Bureau Chief, one Adrian Reef
Said he was sick to the core,
Why wouldn't the weather behave itself
Like it had done before,
'It's making us look like a laughing stock,'
He bitterly said to Jane,
'I want you to ring up the airport now
And charter a small, light plane,'

He loaded the plane up with dry ice
And a generous load of salt,
And lugged along an elephant gun,
The plane took off with a jolt,
He peppered the clouds with ice that day,
He put his job on the line,
The last thing he wanted to have to say:
'The weather is going to be fine.'

And down on the ground at the barbecue
We were sizzling snags and steak,
Having an ice cold beer or two
And trying to stay awake.

The sultry weather was drowsy then
We'd heard the report, in vain,
But just when the steaks were nicely done
It came down, bucketing rain.

We didn't have time to pack it up,
We couldn't save snags or steak,
In only a couple of minutes there
We were staggering round in a lake,
And Oliver's esky floated away
With the rest of the beer we'd bought,
While we took shelter as best we could
Under cover of Maggie's porch.

The water rose right up to our knees,
Our cars were afloat that day,
The chickens drowned and the old hearth hound
Was found seven miles away,
While on the Teev was the Bureau Chief
With a grin that was not quite sane,
He knew he'd won with his elephant gun,
'The sky is threatening rain!'

The Temptation

'I would if I could but I can't,' he said,
'Though I know it would be sublime,
I'm spoken for, and it does my head
To think that you could be mine.
I made a vow, and I don't know how
I could break it, and feel right,
But though I'm true, I'm thinking of you
As I do, each sleepless night.'

He shook his head and he walked away
As she clutched the verandah rail,
She turned her face away when the trace
Of her tears had left a trail.
'I don't know what the attraction is,'
She said, as she wiped her eyes,
'But it must be true what I say to you,
Anything else is lies!'

He walked back into his hotel room
And held his head in his hands,
And as he did the temptation grew
For a taste of contraband.
She'd met him there as she always did
For she serviced all the rooms,
His monthly trip, and her heart would flip
As the day of his coming loomed.

And he would think of her sparkling eyes
The set of her moist, pink lips,
Her flaxen hair and her pointed stare
And the sway of her virgin hips.

Her image was burnt upon his brain
Though he still loved his woman too,
It left him sore and confused, he thought,
What was a man to do?

He fell at last in a deep, deep sleep
And Rhianna entered his room,
She saw him peacefully lying there
Quite unaware in the gloom,
She lay down quiet beside him, just
To see how it felt to lie
Next to the one that her love was on,
He woke, his hand on her thigh.

The silken feel of Rhianna's thigh
Had put him into a trance,
He thought that a dream had come to life
Til he opened his eyes, by chance,
Her lips were hovering over his brow
Her flaxen hair in his face,
Her strange perfume permeated the room,
He rolled off the bed in haste.

'I would if I could but I can't,' he said,
'I need you to understand,
If I were free, with just you and me
But I'm not, and this wasn't planned.'
He left, drove home in the early dawn
To arrive unexpectedly,
And saw the light in the bedroom on,
His woman had company.

She wept as the man had gathered his clothes,
And made poste haste for the door,

While he just stood as if turned to wood,
His feet fast glued to the floor,
'Well, you're always off on your travels, John,
You must consider my plight!'
'That may be so,' as he turned to go,
'But I know where I'll sleep tonight!'

Table Tapping

Some once called him a Grand Old Man,
Others called him a slime,
You couldn't get a consensus that
Was even, all the time,
For some kow-towed to his money, while
Others fell by his sword,
His life was overall sunny, while
His victims quailed at his word.

He lorded it over his children,
He ruled their kids with ease,
A sullen look from beneath his brow
Would bring them to their knees,
His will was forever changing
As solicitors came and went,
One day he'd offer a mansion,
And another day, a tent.

When he finally died he was stony broke
And they wondered where it went,
He'd always been abstemious
But the money had been spent.
He left all their lives in ruins with
Their expectations gone,

A couple of ramshackle houses were
The only things they won.

There wasn't the money to bury him
So they left him where he sat,
Up at the head of the table in
His black, beribboned hat,
He glared at them as he'd glared in life
One hand on the table-top,
Where he used to tap with his finger
As if it would never stop.

Tap-tap-tap on the table-top,
Tap-tap-tap it went,
His eyes bored into the back of your head
As if to say - Repent!
And people scurried, this way and that
To divine what the tartar meant,
The grim old man in his black top hat
Who ruled to their detriment.

They left him sat and they locked the door
Didn't go back for a year,
Til the eldest, saying 'let's know for sure,'
Returned with a tinge of fear.
'He might have stocks in his waistband there
Or shares hid under his shirt,
Or cash stuffed in his beribboned hat -
He treated us all like dirt!'

He ventured into the dining room
Where the grim old man still sat,
His eyes a-glare in the year long gloom
From under the brim of his hat.

But as the eldest approached him there
The finger began to tap,
A steady rap with a note of doom
That would curdle blood to sap.

So Toby dived to the tinder box
And he leapt up with the axe,
His face as pale as a ghostly tale
But determined to attack.
He raised the axe and he let it fall
Severed the finger there,
It skittered across the table top
As the old man fell from his chair.

The stocks were stuffed in the old man's hat
The shares were stuffed in his sleeve,
And so much cash in his waistband that
They said, you wouldn't believe.
But still he's locked in that grey old house
For they found it wouldn't stop,
That severed finger that skittered there
Still taps on the table-top!

The Midnight Plane

His wife was due on the midnight plane
That was coming from Beijing,
He got to the airport early so
He wouldn't miss the thing,
There wasn't a seat at Wenzhou so
He found that he had to stand,
It's always tough when you're sleeping rough
Away, in a foreign land.

He settled down in a corner, set
His back up next to the wall,
Pulled out the pic of his own Mei Ling
In front of a waterfall,
Her eyes smiled into the camera when
He'd taken the snap that day,
But that was before they married,
Now it seemed an age away.

They'd both had to fight her parents when
They saw he was from the west,
They called him a foreign devil, a
Yang wei, and all the rest,
They wanted her wed to a Han, they said,
Mei Ling had answered 'No!'
She'd made her mind up herself, she said,
And would be his own lǎo pó.

She said she was flying China Air
And that gave him cause for thought,
He knew that their safety record was
The worst in any port,
But he waited patiently by the clock
Til it gave the midnight chime,
Then wandered into reception where
She'd be, most any time.

The Chinese waiting beside him
Milled and jabbered as they stood,
He never could understand a word
But he smiled as if he could,
And then he found they were friendly
Though they nudged each other now,

And some had even approached him with
Their greeting, their Ni Hao.

By half past twelve, there wasn't a plane
And the people looked upset,
He thought there'd be an announcement,
Someone said, 'there's nothing yet.'
At one o'clock there were tears and fears
That the plane would never show,
And then he heard that the plane had ditched
In the waters off Ningbo.

His heart had sunk and he almost cried
But he thought to grieve with grace,
And everyone else was struggling
They were scared of 'losing face',
But they all broke down when a man came round
And he said, 'there's little hope,'
There wasn't a single survivor,
Then he cried, he couldn't cope.

He'd lost the love of his life, Mei Ling
With her beaming almond eyes,
Her jet black hair and her loving stare
But he got a quick surprise,
A man led him to a phone where they
Had called for him in vain,
And from Beijing he heard Mei Ling
Who sobbed, 'I missed the plane!'

The Beat of the Drum

It started when he had brought a box
He'd bought, back home from the fair,
The size of an average tinder box
In brass, and embossed with care,
The scene was the site of a battlefield
Where the redcoats marched as one,
In the face of the French artillery
Looking down the mouth of a gun.

And on the right was a drummer boy
Who drummed to the marching feet,
He gazed ahead but his eyes were dead
As he kept up a steady beat,
A moment of peril embossed in time
When nations ruled by the gun,
The redcoats all in a staggered line
With the battle not yet won.

'And how did you come by that,' she said,
His wife, when he brought it home,
'I should know better than let you out
With a pound, when you're on your own.
The gypsies see you abroad, my lad
And they say, 'Now there's our mark!
They'd pick you out of a thousand folk
Out there, a-stroll in the park.'

'It wasn't a gypsy, Jen,' he said,
'But an old, sad military man,
Struggling on a pension for
His bread, as best he can.'

'You're just as soft as the next one, Bill,
They'd steal a beggar's cup,
But now that you've got your tinder box
Let's see, just open it up.'

'I can't, it's locked with a type of lock
That I've never seen before,
It's rusted on, and there is no key,
It's a work of art for sure.'
He set it down by their rustic hearth
Where it looked so very fine,
A piece from their ancient history
Where the soldiers stood in line.

That night they woke to the distant sound
Of a battle, lost and won,
The sound of cheers, of clashes, tears
To the beat of a distant drum,
And Jen was lying there frozen as
She clung to her husband's arm,
'What have you brought on home to us?'
She cried, in her alarm.

The morning saw her attack the lock
With a hammer to no avail,
The lock, it might have been rusty but
Was solid, strong and hale,
And Bill said 'Stop! You will ruin it,
There's nothing there to hide,
I bought it more for the picture than
What might there be inside.'

Each night the sound of a battle filtered
Out of that tinder box,

The sounds of the muskets firing, of
Whizz-bangs and battle shocks,
And through it all was the steady sound
Of the little drummer's beat,
It rose up out of the battleground
With the sound of marching feet.

They finally cut the lock away
With a coarse old hacksaw blade,
It took a couple of hours that day
So sturdy was it made.
Then Bill said 'Your curiosity
Has made me wreck the lock,
So now, there's nothing to stop you, Jen,
Just open up the box.'

The lid flew up and the sight she saw
Was enough to make her faint,
For there, the skull of the drummer boy
Lay with its coat of paint,
And blood, red blood was the skull in there
Though the teeth were pearly white,
A bullet hole in the frontal lobe
That had kissed the boy goodnight.

And folded there, but beneath the skull
Was the skin of the drummer's drum,
Blackened, torn and beyond repair
It had sounded for everyone.
It's buried now with the drummer's skull,
It's resting beneath a tree,
And never sounds, for its war is won,
It's where it was meant to be.

Monsters!

'There are giants out in the hinterland,
There are monsters, horrible frogs,
There are birds of prey out there all day
There are streets of savage dogs.
There are bakers, making their virgin pies
From the girls found out on the street,
I think you'd better stay home and play
For you don't know what you'll meet.'

Janelle sat curled in the corner, with
Her eyes as wide as the moon,
She'd always led such a sheltered life
In a house, as dark as the tomb.
She'd never questioned her father, nor
The dreadful things that he taught,
He told her he was protecting her
For life out there was fraught.

She'd peer on out of the windows, see
The trees that waved in the breeze,
'The sap on the lower branches will
Reach out, and capture your knees.'
She'd hear the wind in its savage bursts
That waited to take her breath,
And wondered why she would have to die
But the world outside was death.

She barely remembered her mother
Who had gone by the age of three,
A wistful smile for a fretful child,
He said she was drowned at sea.

But he often sat by a garden plot
When he said it was safe that day,
And planted a bed of forget-me-nots
To keep grave diggers away.

He'd only leave for a weekly shop
And he'd wear a coat and hat,
Dodging over some fences to
Avoid the giant rat,
The snakes were fierce in the supermart
And he said, 'I do declare,
Don't ever let me forget my hat
Or the bats will get in my hair.'

Janelle would sit by a mirror, and
Despair at her pale, white face,
She rarely got any sun on it
And her body was starting to waste,
Her legs were thin and her arms were skin
And bone, her breasts were small,
Her ribs would show in the mirror's glow
She hadn't much weight at all.

Whenever he'd leave her on her own
He'd be sure to lock the door,
'We don't want the zombies creeping in
And dragging you through the floor!'
He said they lived right under the house
But only came out at night,
And that's when the cats would shriek and yowl,
They put up an awesome fight!

One day he went and forgot to lock,
He must have misplaced the key,

Janelle stood still by the open door
As the wind blew fitfully,
She took a breath, and it wasn't death
But the sweetest of perfume,
The air was laden with scent that day
With the roses in full bloom.

She ventured into the garden, felt
The grass, so soft on her feet,
While the preying birds sat up in the trees,
But all that they did was tweet,
There were no bats, nor a giant rat,
Though a dog came wagging its tail,
And she saw a man in a crimson van
Pull up, delivering mail.

She finally flung her arms up high
In a moment then, and cried,
'The world is wonderful, he was wrong,
He lied,' she said, 'He lied!'
By the time he arrived back home again
Janelle was gone with the wind,
But a policeman stood in his lounge and said,
'At last! Well, do come in!'

Talking Heads

They said it was only climate change,
It would take a hundred years
To raise the temperature one degree,
It was easy to reverse,
But the weather pattern was changing
We could see that for ourselves,
And the strangest things were happening
But it only came in spells.

Torrential rain in the dryest state,
And flooding over the plain,
Blazing heat in the winter like
We'll never see again,
The Ozone Layer had opened up
With the use of C.F.C's,
And the burn effect of the sun increased,
Was causing more disease.

I told Joanne she should cover up
When she sunbathed at the beach,
You can lead a horse to water
But there's some you just can't teach,
She cooked herself to a golden brown
And the burn began to tell,
As the melanomas began to form
In her fragile, human cells.

She had a couple cut out, but then
Some more began to form,
But still she went to the nudist beach
When the sun came up at dawn,

'I want to look brown and healthy
Not a pastey white, like some,'
And shook her head at the zinc cream
And the protection I put on.

The level of radiation was
Increasing with U.V.,
And even the whales in Summer Bay
Got cancers in the sea,
I warned and warned but she tossed her head,
In that stubborn way she had,
I braced myself for the future, for
I knew, it would be bad.

It started off as a scaley lump
On her shoulder, then it grew,
Faster than anything I've seen,
An inch, in a day or two,
I told her to get to the hospital
But she said, 'I'll use some cream.'
We little knew what was coming through
It seemed like a nightmare scene.

She sat in the sun again next day,
I said, 'You're tempting the fates!
Go and have it cut out, Joanne,
Before it gets too late.'
But the clouds rolled up and the sun went in
It was sultry still, not cool,
Then the lightning flashed around our place
And struck, in our garden pool.

It ran along our verandah rail
And it lit up Joanne's chair,

While static electricity
Was crackling in the air,
Her hair stood out like a golliwog
Then her skin began to glow,
And that must have been the moment when
The thing began to grow.

The scab fell off in the morning
Leaving a hole, both red and raw,
And later, when she was screaming,
How to describe the thing I saw?
She stood in front of the mirror with
Her eyes so full of dread,
For up and out of the open wound
Had popped a tiny head.

The tiny head of a pygmy thing
That glared, with razor teeth,
With evil, glittering, crimson eyes
It was just beyond belief,
And then it started to babble in
A strange high, whining tone,
The only words I could understand:
'You'd better leave me alone!'

Joanne collapsed on the bathroom floor
She had gone out like a light,
And I went straight for the cabinet door,
I was petrified with fright,
I pulled out the cut-throat razor and
I sliced it off at the neck,
But not before it had bitten me
As I dropped it on the deck.

I'm writing this final message so
The rest of you will know,
You're going to have to cremate us
To destroy this so-and-so,
Joanne has five, and is terrified
While I have only three,
But we've sliced off more than a dozen heads
So far, God pity me!

Never Come Here Again!

He trudged on up from the great seaport
After a year at sea,
And in his mind was a single thought,
That thought was Emily.
He'd got her note when he disembarked
In the pouring, driving rain,
And read it under a single spark:
'You may never come here again!'

'Never come here again,' it said,
What was that meant to mean?
The blood had rushed to his sailor's head,
He conjured a nightmare scene,
He thought of the tidy garden path,
Of seeing a man at the door,
And Emily hiding behind his hat,
A man he'd not seen before.

Perhaps the year was too long to wait,
She hated it on her own,
He'd often suffered a lack of faith
That she could remain alone.

He'd conjured visions in distant ports
At the curious lack of mail,
While he had written his deepest thoughts
To post them before he sailed.

He'd thought of her at the village dance,
He'd thought of her down the street,
And meeting a friendly guy, perchance
Who would sweep her off her feet.
While he had suffered temptations too
At the taverns along the way,
The sparkling eyes of the barmaids there
When the ship put in for a stay.

But now he trudged in the driving rain
At that terrible time of night,
When shadows loomed to increase the gloom
That he felt, with never a light,
He'd struck a match when he'd read the note
But it fizzled in record time,
He'd only read when the match went out
The first, not the second line.

He felt his way up the garden path
And he paused, then knocked at the door,
His heart was there in his mouth at last
To the tread of a man, for sure.
The door swung open, a man stood there
A quizzical look in his eyes,
'We didn't expect you here so late,
But still, what a nice suprise.'

The sailor stood, was taken aback,
He hadn't the words to say,

'What have you done with Emily,'
His breath was taken away.
'Your Emily's moved, she went next door,
I see she's burning a light,
You'd better get home, you're living there,
She's waiting for you tonight.'

The Duke of Spur

Rosalyn stood in the castle tower
And gazed out over the plain,
It wasn't exactly a sumptuous bower
For the drapes were old, and stained,
The furniture had seen better times
In the days of the knights of old,
But the cracked and broken window panes
Had made the bower cold.

She'd shivered as she had got undressed
And donned a filmy gown,
She pined for the sight she hoped to see
As she stood there, looking down,
Three knights stood guard at the outer moat
Their armour was dull and black,
They couldn't be seen on a moonless night
But were there to ward off attack.

Attack from the southern Baron's men,
Attack from the western marsh,
They came to rescue fair Rosalyn
For her sentence had been harsh,
Confined for life in that wintry tower
For her love for the Duke of Spur,

Who'd not been seen since the winter green,
Nor asked what became of her.

The rain came down in a sudden squall
He shivered, and scratched his head,
What could he do with the Duke of Spur
If the man had turned up dead?
He pushed his seat away from the desk
And he rose, and stretched, and yawned,
The cursor blinked on the final line
As the moon beamed in through the storm.

How could he save fair Rosalyn,
That was the question here,
He opened the door of the old bar fridge
And knocked the head off a beer,
He sat again at the keyboard then
And stared and stared at the screen,
He didn't know where to go from there
But found himself in a dream.

He woke in the damp and windswept tower
Where Rosalyn lay asleep,
He thought that he must be crazy, that
His mind made a giant leap,
He saw the screen in the corner where
He sat, as if in a trance,
But here on the other side of the screen
He was caught, by some mischance.

Rosalyn woke from her slumber then
And she held her arms out wide,
'I wondered when you would join me in
This tale from the other side.

I've seen you sitting and watching me,
You watched as I got undressed,
And I know it's only a story but
In truth, I wasn't impressed.'

'I must be asleep and dreaming,'
He replied, 'but you can't be real,
I haven't finished the story yet
But in here I can see and feel,
And there I am on the other side,
I'm sat in front of the screen.'
'If you don't shut up and make love to me,'
She said, 'then I'm going to scream!'

He spent an hour in a wilful daze,
She held him close in her arms,
He kissed her eyes and her silken thighs
Revealed much more of her charms,
And when they were finally done, she said
'Will you rescue me, or not?'
He lay as dead as he scratched his head,
'I think I've lost the plot!'

He woke as the sun came slowly up
Stiff and cold in his room,
The cursor was dim and blinking as
The only light in the gloom,
He typed that a coil of rope was hid
On the other side of a drape,
Thinking that she could use it then
To make a swift escape.

She saw the rope and she tied it firm
To the leg of the solid bed,

The thought he was going to rescue her
Was the only thought in his head,
She dropped the rope so the Duke of Spur
Could climb and clamber in,
But when he climbed to the window ledge
The Duke of Spur was him!

The Bed & the Wardrobe

I had an Indian Fakir come
To stay, from Uttar Pradesh,
I was doing a friend a favour,
I don't, as a rule, have guests,
I couldn't make out a single word
He said, and so my friend
Provided a written commentary
To guide me, in the end.

It seems he was naming my furniture
It's something that they do,
In places that are incongruous
Like the depths of Kalamazoo,
And he wanted to give them English names
So he asked my friend's advice,
In case I couldn't pronounce them,
Well, at least the thought was nice.

My armchair became Albert
And my settee Gunga Din,
I suppose he thought it would be okay
As it *was* from Kipling.
The tallboy was called Gerald
And the wardrobe, simply Joe,

The polished table Cheryl
And the kitchen one was Flo.

I'm glad that he wrote them down because
I can't remember names,
Just that the bed was Susan
And the kitchen sink was James,
Some of them were portentous like
Ignatius, for the desk,
While each of the kitchen chairs was given
A name that ends with -este.

Celeste, Impreste, Doneste and Geste
And then of course, Ingeste,
I couldn't remember which was which,
My friend was not impressed.
We bade farewell to the Fakir
And the Wardrobe flapped its doors,
And rumbled out a 'Goodbye my friend'
From between its mighty jaws.

Then voices rose in a chorus from
Each part of my tidy home,
The names had given them each a voice,
It was rowdier than Rome,
The voices were accusatory
Trying to lay some guilt,
And Susan said of the Wardrobe, Joe,
'He's looking up my quilt!'

'How could I help it,' Joe replied,
'I'm at the foot of the bed,
You're flashing me with your silken sheets,
It's doing in my head!'

While Albert grumbled in voice so deep,
'Do I have to be a chair?
Each time you plonk on my tender seat
I'm gasping out for air!'

Then the kitchen chairs were out of place
And James was choked with suds,
The carpet, name of Emily
Was sick of traipsing mud.
It seemed that the polished table top
Was scratched, and she was mad,
The desk disliked my keyboard so
To each, I answered 'Sad!'

'You're going to have to get along
I won't put up with this,
Until that Fakir came along
This house was perfect bliss.'
I did away with their English names,
Replaced them with Chinese,
But they couldn't speak a word of it
So I brought them to their knees!

And peace returned to Grissom Place
Just as I thought it would,
I made it plain to Wardrobe Joe
'You're just a lump of wood.'
While Susan smooths her quilt right down
And tucks her sheets right in,
And James just blubs, he's full of suds
As I nap on Gunga Din!

Girl on a Train

He had got on the train at New Street,
Found an empty carriage spare,
And settled down with the paper
With not one to disturb him there,
But the train pulled in at Sandwell
And the carriage door slid wide,
And in there walked a pair of heels
With a dimple and hips beside.

She sat on the seat across from him
And laid her bag on the seat,
Kicked her shoes on the floor, so he
Could see her pretty feet,
He tried to look at his paper but
The print got up and walked,
Up from her ankles to her calfs
And he found it hard to talk.

'How do you do,' was banal but
That's all that came to mind,
She briefly looked from her knitting, and
He thought that her eyes were kind,
But never a word would pass those lips
She had the slightest pout,
And her needles clicked to the railway clack
As his mouth was drying out.

He'd bought some fruit in the Bullring
So he thought he'd have some there,
And at different times he offered her
An apple, peach or a pear,

But she shook her head so slightly and
Politely, in disdain,
As if the thought of a stranger's fruit
From a man in a suit, might stain.

The train chuffed on through Wolverhampton
While he drank a Coke,
He knew that his time was limited
For she'd get off at Stoke,
He offered to put the window down
But she said it blew her hair,
Then he offered his name as Paul, but she
Was not inclined to share.

She crossed her legs and she hitched her skirt
Just slightly above her knees,
While his eyes looked up to the luggage rack,
Was this some sort of tease?
Her knitting needles were clicking away
Was she knitting some sort of sack?
It seemed like she was racing the train
Ahead of its clickety-clack.

The train went racing to Stafford,
In and out, but it passed so fast,
He said, 'We're almost at Stoke, that's where
We'll both get out, I guess?
There's quite a nice little café
Down by the station in the square,
I'd like to buy you a coffee, if you want
I'll shout you there.'

She stopped, and packed up her knitting
Tucked it carefully in her bag,

And said, 'You must be Australian,
And coming here, so sad.
I've never been 'shouted' a drink before
But I think you're rather nice,
I'll let you know that you're past first base
On your way to Paradise!'

McAvanagh's Hill

Alan had stood at our open door,
Shaking and white with fright,
First he was speaking to Eleanor,
Then had a word with Dwight.
'What seems the problem,' I said to him,
(My name, by the way, is Bill),
'Haven't you seen it,' he said to me,
'It's moving, McAvanagh's Hill!'

I went to the door and I looked on out,
The hill seemed to still be in place,
On closer inspection, it seemed to me
It had moved to the south, a trace.
'It must be a trick of the light,' I said,
A hill is a hill and can't move,'
'But look at McCafferty's,' Alan said,
'It's settling down in a groove.'

And true, but McCafferty's roof had moved,
It used to stand up on the height,
The moon would come up just behind his roof
And highlight his house every night.
His house had dropped down the back of the hill
Or the top of the hill was too high,

'Now isn't that strange?' I said in a muse,
And Dwight said, 'I wonder why?'

The rumbling, grumbling started that night
But deep in the earth, underneath,
And Eleanor came in a panic to cry,
'There's movement, out there on the heath!'
We ran to the garden, and under the moon
We could see the heath starting to tilt,
As slowly it moved, and then it became
The rising front side of the hill.

Alan ran home and brought back a gun
He said, 'I feel better with this!'
'You think you can stop it by firing a gun?'
'At least with a hill, you can't miss.
There's something behind it, something so weird,
A hill can't just move by itself.'
Then Eleanor suddenly burst into tears,
'The Devil's come into the Dell!'

We didn't get very much sleep that night,
We took it in turns just to watch,
The nearer the movement came up to our door
The more Alan knocked off my Scotch.
We felt the first tilt of the house next day,
Our porch was beginning to rise,
The hill loomed above us, and leaning back,
The house pointed up to the skies.

McCafferty's house had quite disappeared
As it slid down the other side,
While our house was on the way to the top,
It was really a question of pride.

McCafferty lorded it over us all
As long as his house was on top,
But now he came racing along, was appalled,
'I order this movement to stop!'

'I know you're behind it, you've conjured a scheme,
What set this in motion, Bill?'
I shrugged and I mentioned that my hands were clean,
'It is, after all, just a hill!'
'My real estate value just fell through the floor,
I'll sue if you don't move it back!'
'Then go for it Buddy, there isn't a court
That can order a hill… See you Jack.'

We're sitting in clover, our house at the top
Of what was McAvanagh's Hill,
For once it had moved, it suddenly stopped
And now it's the Hill of Bill!
McCafferty sits down the hill in a glade
And he rages at everyone,
While Alan's deluded, he swears at this stage
That it stopped when it noticed his gun.

The Naked Lady of Houghton Hall

Houghton Hall had been derelict
Since the Roundheads came and went,
They said that it couldn't be restored
No matter how much you spent,
But I loved that place and its spacious grounds
So I went against advice,
I paid a pittance and thought I'd get
A part of it looking nice.

It still had the stately central stair,
It still had the marble floors,
It needed a bit of the lead replaced
But still had the cedar doors.
The windows needed a scrub and clean
Were original pebble glass,
It soon was done though my Bank was lean
And I moved right in, at last.

There wasn't much furniture at first
To muffle its ancient walls,
My footsteps echoed around the floors
Of its entry, rooms and halls,
It was only then that I saw her walk
In the gloom of a winter's night,
And found I'd bought, along with the Hall
A ghostly woman in white!

She glided along the balustrade
Came steadily down the stair,
I stood well back in the entryway
Pretended I wasn't there.

Then she stopped and grabbed at the bannister
And let out a dreadful wail,
It seemed to swell from the hounds of hell
And I felt myself grow pale.

She seemed to fade on the stairway there
And her wailing went as well,
The hair stood up on the back of my neck
For I felt she'd come from hell.
So I asked around with the village folk
If they knew, they said they might,
And for a bribe of a drink or two
Described the woman in white.

It seems she had been Lord Houghton's bride
When the Roundheads came to call,
And Ireton's men had shot the Lord,
He told them to kill them all.
She died on the central stairway there
She died from a single shot,
While the Roundheads plundered the ancient hall
With her corpse left there to rot.

I felt for her, yes, I really did
It was such a gory tale,
But it got too much when at night I hid
For she came each night to wail.
My eyes were haggard, I couldn't sleep
I was feeling so uptight,
And then I came across the cupboard
That clothed the woman in white.

The cupboard stood in an upstairs room
That I hadn't quite restored,

I hadn't bothered for in the gloom
The damp had swollen the door,
And in a drawer was a pile of clothes
So old, that she kept for best,
And there preserved with a bullet hole
Was the very same woman's dress.

I took the dress and I hid it well,
Then waited for her that night,
Till she came stumbling down the stair,
She did, the woman in white.
But there was no sign of the dress on her
Just camiknickers in silk,
And pain and sadness were in her wail
Though her skin was white as milk.

A week went by and she still came down
That stairway to keen and wail,
So I went back with my sleepless frown
And I hid it, without fail,
The camiknickers, the stockings, shoes
And I left that cupboard bare,
Invited a crowd from the local hunt
To come, to stand and stare.

And she came just once on that fateful night
She was naked and serene,
Then she saw us all in the entryway
And the woman stood and screamed.
If you need to get rid of a troublesome ghost
You must cause some slight mishap,
She never came back down the stairs again
Once we all just stood, and clapped.

The Watcher

The change in his habits was hard to define,
He thought, getting older, had shortened his time,
Less time to waste sleeping, for rest or respite,
From eight hours to six hours, to four hours at night.

He'd sit up late working, and not watch the clock
At midnight he'd vaguely hear something tick-tock,
But still would sit up with his eyes full of rue
And not get to bed until one, maybe two.

Awake before dawn he would feel some relief,
That death had not squandered his life in his sleep,
And though he was tiring, he wouldn't give in,
Began to see sleeping as some kind of sin.

Then down to an hour, and then to a half
He ended up napping short time by the hearth,
Five minutes would pass, he'd be fully awake
When under his chair he would feel the earth quake.

And when his eyes opened and looked to the skies
He'd see giant gimbals above the sunrise,
That held the earth spinning in place like a top
A gyroscope, seeming it never would stop.

Then in the dark hours when all were asleep,
He'd see all the monsters come out for a peep,
Come out from their hidings in forest and glen
Whenever they hadn't to fear meeting men.

They'd play in the shallows, they'd play in the streams,
They'd dash in and out of the sleeping mens dreams,
They'd laugh and they'd frolic up high in the trees,
And wave in the branches with every slight breeze.

And sometimes they'd argue, and sometimes they'd fight,
Hip-hopping from one to the other all night,
They'd not see the watcher, awake in his den
For monsters see horrors in all kinds of men.

The world would return to the way it had been
Before men came begging, and made it unclean,
With meadows and grotto's and magical spells,
And hedgerows and sedge rows and woods of bluebells.

He sat there in wonder, and watched the full flight
Of worlds unimagined that came out each night,
And suddenly death was the least he would fear
If death would come dreaming and carry him there.

The watcher relaxed and he fell sound asleep
He slept for eight hours with never a peep,
And when he awoke with the rise of the sun,
He wept in his sorrow, what sleep had undone.

Jonathon's Dilemma

The world looks grim when your eyes are dim
And they're swollen red with tears,
When all that you've won has come undone
And all you have left are fears,
So Jonathon Ley had felt that day
When he looked for his missing girl,
But she was several streets away
In bed with a man called Earl!

His world had come to a shuddering end,
His hopes had burst at the seams,
He knew that his heart would never mend
And all he had left were dreams.
The clouds of grief that came like a thief
Had stolen his girl, Elaine,
And she, the source of his one belief
Was promising only pain.

He hadn't had any back-up plans
When planning his life ahead,
With Lainey gone he was on his own
Just him, and his empty head,
He thought that he'd put an end to it
The pain and suffering; How?
He spent some days considering ways
Under his furrowed brow.

He climbed to the top of the Town Hall clock
And found himself looking down,
All that he had to do was drop
Right next to the Lost & Found,

He'd looked on up from the street below
Took a final look at a star,
But didn't know when he had to go
That the street would be down so far.

There's always time for a change of plan
He thought, as he climbed back down,
Hiding his face from everyone
In case they thought him a clown.
He took a blade from the kitchen drawer
And thought he'd go to the park,
Then slit his throat in his overcoat,
By God, but that blade was sharp!

He wandered moping along the street
To think just what could be done,
He wanted to do it, quick and neat
But he hadn't bought him a gun,
Then Lainey came, she had changed her mind
For Earl was a dog, and things,
'You got the jist of the story wrong,
He asked me to test his springs!'

So Jonathon's world came back in view
The clouds were cleared from his sky,
With everything now about her new
He never asked Lainey why.
They wed in June, in the afternoon
And the baby came in a whirl,
But he wouldn't presume to question why
The baby looked like Earl!

Gulp! – (Lol)

I wrote a book called 'The Afterdeath'
With a thousand gory themes,
Of what takes place at your final breath
When you lie in your swirling dreams,
Your body hung by its fingertips
Between here and the place you go,
When the deed is done, and your race is run
Will there be no afterglow?

Will there be no afterglow, I said
With a place you can lay your head,
Up in the clouds and the stars somewhere
On a downy, cloudy bed?
To wake from the sordid human dream
That you lived, three score and ten,
Trying to make your way between
Your hopes and ambitions then.

But always thwarted, you don't know why
For nothing would come out right,
And always hanging over your head
Are thoughts of that endless night,
That bright intelligence snuffed right out
That learning lost to the air,
Your body locked in a six foot box
In its final death despair.

I wrote of the ones who wake in dread
To the sound of the shovel's spray,
Tipping that final dirt on you
As your coffin's hidden away,

You thump and scream in your final dream
Kicking the bottom out,
With the coffin muffling shrieks and screams
When you want them to let you out!

It's easy, while I am sitting here
To write of a man's despair,
When he's in the dark, can't see a spark
And fighting for gasps of air,
Or maybe rather the sputtering jets
Of the crematorium,
As the box implodes and your body glows
Round your scared cerebellum?

So now that I've made you comfortable
Accepting your sad demise,
And the way that they will dispose of you
(Believe me, everyone lies!)
Take heart in the fact you're not alone
That final terror will be
There at the end with everyone,
Including the author, Me!'

The Gargoyle

Back in the tiny town of Hamm
In a province best unknown,
Is an ancient sandstone prison tower
Where the grounds are overgrown.
The locals still in the town are few
Were wary of us at first,
But ventured out when they heard me shout
To tell me the tower was cursed.

'Don't venture there if you fear despair,'
They said in a foreign tongue,
Then slunk back, each to his rundown lair,
But we were too smart, and young.
'They're peasants, what would they know,' said Kym,
'They're superstitious and fools,
We'll test their funny old tower now.'
We should have played by their rules.

It was built in a grim and Gothic style
But had sadly been run down,
Hundreds of years of standing there
Put a torpor over the town.
The rusty railings, falling apart
Had never been breached by them,
The peasants whispered and looked away
In the manner of Holy men.

We made our way through the bushes, sedge
And weeds that grew in the grounds,
But then up close to the building saw
Some features that astound.

The walls had flying buttresses,
A door with a pointed arch,
And a gargoyle leering from above
Next to soldiers on the march.

We didn't go in the first time there
But wandered around the site,
It was Kym who had the bright idea
We should go and explore by night.
I wish that we'd known its history
For that might have broken its spell,
I wouldn't have sought its mystery,
And Kym would still be well.

We noticed an old Teutonic sign
Engraved, and above the door,
We couldn't translate it at the time
It should have been done before;
Before we entered that cursèd place
And risking our sanity,
For I came out with a twisted face
Though Kym was worse than me.

The moon was casting a yellow glow
As we stood before that door,
Directly under the gargoyle that
Let out a fearful roar,
Then a stream of ectoplasm flowed
From its jaws, and down on Kym,
Covered her in this bluish light
And then, it dragged her in.

I followed, not that I had a choice
I was quite beyond control,

My legs did whatever they wanted to,
I had no choice at all.
Inside was a vaulted ceiling over
An old and blood-stained block,
And Kym was struggling, screaming,
As she was stretched across its top.

She glowed and glowed in this bluish light
Her neck was placed on the block,
And then a shimmering man appeared
I think I went into shock.
He held a shining scimitar sword
And he raised it up to strike,
And still I live that terrible scene,
Each and every night.

I saw it clearly pass right through
The base of Kym's long neck,
And watched as this bluish head fell off
Went rolling along the deck.
But her head was there, was still in place
As I dragged her screaming out,
It was then I noticed my twisted face
That I can do nothing about.

They say that it's called Bell's Palsy, that
I must have suffered a shock,
The right hand side of my face is numb,
My eye and my mouth have dropped,
But Kym just utters the weirdest moans
As if blood was starved from her brain,
Her eyes astare at the horror there
I think she must be insane.

The last I saw of that evil tower
The gargoyle seemed to grin,
As if to say there is hell to pay
For those who might come right in.
And the screed engraved above the door
The letters were filled with lead,
'You've come to the Tower of Grimm von Gore,
Enter, and lose your head!'

In A Poem's Wake

I'm hot on the tail of a poem's trail
To discover what makes it tick,
For the ones I receive in the daily mail
Are always giving me stick.
I don't want the ones with a psycho-probe
That go ravelling into my brain,
Or a moody muse with a too short fuse
They only generate pain.

When I spot one bearing a carefree lilt,
A rhythm that echoes my heart,
Or a rhyme scheme pairing a seem with dream,
We're off to a flying start.
It gallops ahead of me, feeling its way
Through words that it finds by chance,
And makes it plain that it wants to play
In the meadows of assonance.

So I chase it over a babbling brook
On a cliché, rhyme or hook,
And still the breeze that will rhyme with trees
Turns the pages of my book.

I search for characters, sweet young girls
And for ladies, fair of face,
Who dance along with the poem, twirl
In the aftermath of grace.

While men, the heroes of quests and seas
Marooned on a distant shore,
Will take the poem to where they please,
You've never been there before.
And they meet the girls with the hair like corn,
Are trapped in their sparkling eyes,
They come together in winter storm
And all that you hear are sighs.

For the poem gives, and the poem takes
It will lull you, thrill you, dance,
From its wedding bells to its funeral wakes
It will still you, fill, entrance!
Its magic lies in its rhyme and scheme
As it weaves a recurring spell,
It nestles into your heart and dreams
Like an Olde Tyme Wishing Well.

And when it finally comes to stand
On the shore of a timeless lake,
As the book slips out of your listless hand
It whispers, 'Are you awake?'
Then I spring to life and I seize it then,
And give to its tail a twist,
'I'm still the poet, I hold the pen,'
I write, in the evening mist!

Double Jeopardy

It was always a hassle on Fridays
To sort my weekends out,
If Angela said, 'Those are *my* days,'
Then it left me in no doubt.
I would have to travel to Moira,
Come up with a good excuse,
'I couldn't drive to the north, my dear,
I have a wheel bearing loose!'

So I'd have to put the car on a jack
And then unscrew the wheel,
Take my time in putting it back
I had to make it real.
Then Monday kissing her and the kids
A fond and a long goodbye,
'Make sure you wear your bicycle lids,
I'll see you, bye and bye.'

And Angela would welcome me home
She'd had a rough weekend,
She'd taken the kids to their grandma's, then
Had tended a sickly friend.
We had three days to rumple the bed
Until I had to go,
Arriving back at Moira's, just in time
To take in a show.

It wasn't a set routine because
It varied from week to week,
Angela was the stay-at-home,
Moira the dancing freak,

I'd married Angey at twenty-one
For she loved to stay at home,
And Moira, wed just five years on
Who always wanted to roam.

I managed to keep the two apart
And I led a varied life,
A quiet romp with the stay-at-home,
A fling with my roaming wife,
But the kids had come, with three for one,
And two for the other half,
And what once seemed the perfect dream
Became an ironic laugh.

Lucky I had a well-paid job,
Lucky I held it down,
Keeping the one a stay-at-home
While the other raged in town,
I thought I must be the only one
To have complicated my life,
But that was until a man called Bill
Spoke of his second wife.

He must have been drunk, he said he was
Or he wouldn't have said a thing,
He said that it only started off
As a mad, misguided fling,
He'd met the first in a ladies bar,
And she'd gone to his lonely bed,
It became a loose, irregular thing
And before he knew, was wed.

She always wanted to gad about,
She never would stay at home,

He got so sick of the nightclub clique
That he lost the will to roam.
He met another who liked to sit
And cuddle up by his side,
And in a moment of madness then
She became his second bride.

'It seems to work, but it's hard to plan
For they both have days away,
I have to coordinate my time
With the one that's free that day.'
'The same with me, I'm never free,
I haven't sufficient time,
When I want a quiet night at home
She wants to dance the line.'

A week went by since our talk, and I
Was sat in the Scarlet Lounge,
Waiting for Moira to come by
When I spotted Bill with Ange!
They walked right by, and I heard a sigh
As Bill saw Moira Freeze,
I hid behind a pillar as Ange
Went off by herself to sneeze.

I waited till she was on her own
Then went and confronted Ange,
'What are you doing here, my dear,
Here in the Scarlet Lounge?
You always wanted to stay at home
Are you on your own out here?'
While Bill on the other side of the lounge
Was questioning Moira dear.

So Moira was Bill's quiet one
While she led me quite a dance,
And Ange, who was my stay-at-home
Was going with him to prance!
We thought that we were the bigamists
But it's left us in some doubt,
We think that they may be trigamists
On the days that we're both shut out!

To Bed! To Bed!

'To bed! To bed!'
Said Sleepy-head;
'Tarry awhile,' said Slow;
'Put on the pan,'
Said Greedy Nan;
'We'll sup before we go.'

    (from Mother Goose)

They sat at the kitchen table as
The candle flickered low,
And Greedy Nan put on the pan
To indulge her sister, Slow,
While Sleepy Weepy Annabelle
Blotted her book with tears,
And thought of her Beau from long ago
Who she hadn't seen for years.

'Why doesn't Roger notice me,
Why doesn't Alan Dell?
I'm wearing the dress cut low for me
And I've hitched my skirt as well.
I've a pretty turn to my ankle, so
You'd think it would drive them wild.'

'But men are a mystery,' said Slow,
'And Alan Dell's a child.'

While over the pan stood Greedy Nan,
Was cracking a turkey's egg,
A lump of yeast and a slice of beast
And a single spider's leg.
With a wing of bat and an ounce of fat
And a toe of frog for the spell,
She needed to turn her sister off
From her crush on Alan Dell.

For Greedy Nan was the eldest girl
And would have to marry first,
The other two would wait in the queue
Or their fortunes be reversed,
The omelette sizzled, and in the pan
She added before they saw,
A piece of some Devil's Trumpet plant
For the mating game meant war.

She sliced the omelette into half
And she served them up a piece,
'Didn't you want?' said Annabelle
But Slow enjoyed the feast.
'I'm not that terribly hungry now
I've cooked it up in the pan,
I think I'll just have a slice of bread,'
Said the scheming Greedy Nan.

They finished up and they sat awhile,
And they mused about their fate,
'If Greedy Nan isn't married soon,
For us it will be too late.'

'I've set my sights on a country squire,'
Said Nan, without a blink,
Lured them away from her secret fire
To confuse what they might think.

'The room is woozy, spinning around,
I'd better get me to bed,'
Said Annabelle, while Slow with a frown
Saw Dwarves dancing in her head.
But Greedy Nan was cleaning the pan
To clear all signs of the spell,
Her back was turned to her sisters, spurned
For the sake of Alan Dell.

And when he came in the morning
Greedy Nan was sat by the door,
While Annabelle and her sister Slow
Were lying dead on the floor,
'I didn't mean it to kill them, Al,
It was only a simple spell,'
But as he cuffed and led her away
He frowned, did Alan Dell.

The Blank Page

I've kept a journal of sorts for years
And I enter it in ink,
Not with a ball-point biro, it's
Designed to make me think.
I form the letters with loving care
And I use an italic pen,
And keep it safe on a shelf up where
I can read it, over again.

The journal contains my deepest thoughts,
My secrets, hidden away,
Not to be seen by the eyes of men
Till I'm under the earth one day,
For all the wrongs that I didn't right
And the rights that I failed to do,
Are hidden within its pages in
A sort of italic stew.

So when I received a letter from
A woman called Columbine,
Who said after reading my journal
She could never, ever be mine,
She mentioned a certain entry that
Had made up her mind, she said,
But the time and the stamp on the envelope
Was dated a year ahead.

I never had heard of a Columbine,
I didn't know who she was,
But the fact that she'd read my journal
Made me more than a little cross.

I went to the shelf that held my book
To see what I had to thank,
But the page that she had quoted from
Was an empty page, a blank.

I went one day to the library
To look for a book of mine,
And the girl behind the counter there
Had a name tag, Columbine.
I looked deep into her stark black eyes
At the fall of her lustrous hair,
At her pouting lips and her fingertips,
And all I could do was stare.

She stamped my book and she stared at me
And she saw me staring back,
'Is there anything else that I can do?'
She said, and called me Jack.
'How do you know my name?' I said,
'Well that's not super hard!'
And then she handed my book to me,
'It's on your library card!'

I asked her out for a meal, and then
The rest is history,
We were just engaged when I got to the page
That she'd written about to me.
I raised the pen, and decided then
That I had too much to thank,
Put the cap on my pen, and then
Left all the pages blank.

The Reversal

I was sitting outside the house at dawn
Having a quiet smoke,
I'm never allowed to smoke inside
And I'm just a quiet bloke,
I watched the first few friendly rays
Of the sun, rise over the town,
But then it grew dark, I watched amazed
As the sun went slowly down.

So dark, as black as a midden
And I truly felt alarmed,
Our cockerel ran in a circle, then
Fell down, was somehow charmed.
Surely the earth had not reversed,
But my senses said it had,
And when my chair went floating,
Then I knew that the news was bad.

Everything that was not tied down
Had slowly begun to rise,
Even my car and the outside bar
Hovered before my eyes,
I suddenly felt as light as air
And I had to grab a pole,
While the neighbour's mobile home took off
And left behind a hole.

I made my way to the bedroom then,
It was doing in my head,
And there was the wife, still sound asleep
Floating above the bed,

The quilt and blankets were floating too
And I tried to hold them down,
'I didn't think that you cared,' she said
As she woke, with a puzzled frown.

The problem lasted for seven hours
While we floated round inside,
I made my way to the ceiling light
And repaired the one that died.
The milk flew off from the cereal
And the toast popped up to the roof,
'You see, the earth has reversed,' I said,
'If you need it, there's the proof!'

The news was coming in fits and starts
From the station in the town,
While men were bracing beneath the desk
Just to hold the anchor down,
'A giant comet has hit the earth
And has spun it in reverse,
They say that it's only temporary,
Still, it could be worse.'

At midday, there was a glimmer of light
As the sun began to rise,
The furniture settled down again
And we saw familiar skies,
But the seven hours that we lost will be
Quarantined from time,
Unless we want to be rising as
The Noonday bells will chime.

And one thing that was a certainty
We'll never trust again,

We said, 'As sure as the sun comes up…'
But that was way back when.
And now I notice our cockerel
Can't seem to sing a note,
Since ever its doodle-doodle-cock
Came backwards from its throat.

In Search of the Woman Thing

We came in through the undergrowth
To a patch of blasted trees,
Then checked the radiation that
Had brought earth to its knees,
The skyscrapers were gaunt and tall
They rose like a cankered cell,
Of shattered forms, all overgrown
With a weed spawned straight from hell.

Then Roach said that we should wait awhile,
Make sure it had stabilised,
We'd seen what happened to men before
When they glowed, before our eyes,
But that had been thirty years before,
When men had made mistakes,
We'd not seen a man since we began
Living on rats and snakes.

I vaguely recalled the woman thing
That had held me in her arms,
Who cooed and cried when the lightning died
And the bells shrieked in alarm,
But we hadn't seen a woman thing
For years, for they all died out,

It was something to do with ovaries
And things we don't know about.

We'd met as a pair of ragamuffins
Roaming over the plains,
Hiding under a hollow tree
To avoid the acid rains,
Our skin was scarred, and our life was hard
But we managed to survive,
And now, as far as we knew we were
The only men alive.

I knew she'd read from the Bible for
That was a woman thing,
She taught me plenty of words back then
And showed me scribbling,
So I read fragments to Roach who said
He'd had something called a sis,
I had a piece of a Bible, torn
That was just called Genesis.

We smiled at the thought of a world that was
Quite empty, just as now,
But set in a fabulous garden with
A God, we'd find somehow,
And in there was the name of a man
My woman thing gave to me,
And while he slept, the God man kept
A rib, and he called it Eve.

The city that lay before us may
Have well been Babylon,
But silent now and deserted with
Its ancient people gone,

We wandered into its cluttered streets
And we saw the things of men,
All scaled with rust and a loss of trust
It would never come again.

It was there that we found a woman thing
Who was scarred, and scared as well,
For she'd never seen a man before
And thought that we'd come from hell,
She sat, backed into a corner,
And begging us both to leave,
But I said I was known as Adam, so
She must have been known as Eve.

And then that night, we had a fight
I committed a mortal sin,
I killed my friend as he went to bend
Over the woman thing,
And God roared out with his thunder,
I would always be to blame,
And then decreed in my hour of need
I would call my first son Cain.

The Cuckoo's Nest

They lived in a farm on the lower slopes
Of a place called Gresty Hill,
Three sisters, Emily Jane and Hope
And the younger one called Jill,
My father said to avoid those girls
And my mother echoed him,
'They're plain and nasty and not for you,
My son, my darling Jim.'

Like everything that's denied to you
My interest was aroused,
I'd watch them swilling the pigs below
And milking the Jersey cows,
They went barefoot and they slopped through mud,
When they laughed, I heard their cries,
And watched from up on the hill above
Till I caught their laughing eyes.

Then they'd point at me, and they'd strut and flounce
And would shake their tangled hair,
A blonde, brunette and an auburn girl
They would stand below, and stare,
And sometimes, when they were feeling bold
They would hitch their skirts up high,
Put one foot on a water cask
And show me a muddy thigh.

'Don't never go down to that Gresty Farm,'
My parents made me swear,
'For once they get you they'll use their charm
And will likely keep you there.'

But the girl called Jill had a butter churn
And she made it soft as silk,
And came with Hope to our rustic barn,
Selling the sisters' milk.

They smiled and giggled when I came out
And they thrust their wares at me,
'I don't know whether the folks will want,'
I said, 'I'll go and see.'
But my father came and shooed them off,
'We don't want the likes of you!
You keep yourselves to your Gresty Farm
And do what you have to do.'

I asked my mother what they had done
And she shed a whispy tear,
'Some things cannot be undone, my son,
I try not to interfere.'
My father turned to me, stony, grim
Said sleeping dogs should lie,
'The likes of them are forbidden, Jim,
But you'll not know the reason why.'

The day came after my father fell
From the tractor, over the hill,
Was crushed, and after the funeral
All of his secrets spilled.
My mother took me aside to say
That my father wasn't a saint,
'You know how a cuckoo drops its egg
In another's nest... Don't faint!'

'Two of the three at Gresty Farm
Were his, but I don't know which,

Their widowed mother would put about
Before they were born, the bitch!
It well could be the first and the third,
The second, I couldn't tell,
All I know is your father made my
Life, like a living hell!'

Jim went down to the Gresty Farm
For the first time in his life,
He lined up three of the Gresty girls
And said, 'I need me a wife.
I'm told that two of the three of you
Are my sisters, is it true?
I need to know what your mother knows
For I sure can't marry two.'

Their mother Gail gave a fearsome wail
When confronted by the four,
The daughters said, 'Well we never knew,
Why didn't you tell us before?'
'Emily Jane and Hope were his,
I never was going to tell,
But Jill was William Parson's girl,
Your father should burn in hell!'

He took Jill back to his hillside farm
And he called his mother out,
'This is Jill, and her father's Bill,
I've been told that, without doubt.'
Then he said to Jill, 'Will you marry me?'
She was coy, and answered slow,
'You'll have to prove you can carry me,
If you can, you never know!'

The Witch of Willow Vale

'There's a crafty witch in Willow Vale
Putting spells on all the men,
She lures them out with a lurid tale
Of what they might miss, and then…
She chews them up and she spits them out
And they go home looking pale,
She just wants to prove to fretful wives
That she governs all things male.'

Pamela stood in the door and paused
And she looked direct at me,
'If you should fall for her witches charms
You can go, I'll set you free!
I'll not take seconds from lovesick men
Who come when the witch is through,
You'll not come in through my door again,
That's right, I'm looking at you!'

So I threw my hands up in the air
And I said, 'Why pick on me?
Have I so much looked at a scheming witch
When she's up to her deviltry?'
'That may be true but your time is due
You're the last one in the Glen,
She'll get to you when she sees you're new
For a perfect score of ten.'

'I promise Pamela, I'll be true,'
But she said to call it quits,
'An easy promise that you can't keep
Is a lie upon your lips.'

Then I got mad and I said I'd had
Being judged up front, was lame,
I said I'd travel to Willow Vale
Play the witch at her own game.

'Well just remember that if you do
A touch is all it will take,
A simple kiss that will bring you bliss
That would be your first mistake.
Don't think you might get away with it
For I have my little spies,
I even know how the spell will grow
If you look deep into her eyes.'

So I set off for the witch's haunt
In a cottage, in the vale,
And hearing Pamela's final taunt
'You won't live to tell the tale!'
I pursed my lips, and gritted my teeth
As I knocked on the witch's door,
It swung out wide, to show her sat
By a cauldron on the floor.

She didn't even look up at me
She was sorcering a spell,
Dropping roots in the cauldron there
And muttering as they fell,
Her hair fell over her shoulders and
Her face was in the shade,
And then she stopped and she looked at me
'Did you come here to get laid?'

I blushed and stammered and caught my breath,
This wasn't going well,

My blood was running as cold as death
As I fell beneath her spell.
She'd painted her lips and eyelids black
And her fingernails like claws,
She said, 'I'm ready to claw your back
You need only say, 'I'm yours!''

Her dress she slid up above her knees
To reveal her silken thighs,
Her bodice open, she leaned right back
And I had to shut my eyes.
'I came to tell you you're not for me,
That you weave your spells in vain,
I have a love that is true, you see
I don't need to play your game.'

She bounded up to her feet and cried
'A kiss for a lonely witch!
I'm only asking a single kiss,
What could be wrong with this?'
I shook my head and I turned to go,
And I reached for the cottage door,
Then the wig came off and I heard her laugh,
And there lay Pam, on the floor!

An Old Love

We never forget the ones we loved
If the feeling was strong and true,
No matter what happened, the push and shove
That separates me from you,
And those who came after, who took your place
Will never extinguish the spark,
That sits in the memory's starkest place
After making new love in the dark.

For an old love's more than a pretty face,
It's more than a bunch of sighs,
It's more than a fragile cobweb's grace
That recalls the look in your eyes,
It sits together with faded youth
We recall on our darkest nights,
The pain, obsession, the laughter too
As the mirror of memory lights.

The further down we push it away
It comes when we least expect,
Bustling in from our salad days
With a feeling of sad neglect,
How did it stutter and how did it fail
Is the question that meets our eyes,
And then we remember the truth of it,
Our false and our feeble lies.

Whatever possessed us to stray back then
We made up the perfect two,
But you would get angry with me, my love,
And I would get angry with you,

So our footsteps strayed and we lost the way
To find our way home again,
I'd be with girls that I didn't know
And you'd be with other men.

But we're still back there in the years that fled
And we'll be together again,
When people talk of the life we led
In that time of way back when,
There are certain times in my history
That I see as a strange purview,
When I was entranced by your mystery,
And you were just simply you.

The Grotto

We had come across this grotto in
The cliff near Cater's Pride,
And were swimming in the shallows
When we took a look inside,
There was just a tiny entrance that
Had broadened to a hall,
And the strange effect of lighting seemed
Reflected off each wall.

There were seashells, there were gemstones
Shining, in the rocky face,
And a narrow path around a pool
With depths we could not trace,
But the water was so clear and blue,
And warm, it must be said,
That Cathy cried, 'Can this be true?'
While I just shook my head.

We sat back on the ledge and dangled
Feet down in the blue,
We didn't know that danger loomed
And nor, I think, would you,
But then some minor turbulence
Disturbed the perfect pool,
And suddenly three heads appeared
To laugh, and play the fool.

Three nymphs with sparkling eyes and teeth
Who splashed, their laughter pealed
And echoed round the grotto, as
Their presence was revealed,
They saw us and they beckoned us
As if to swim and play,
If only caution reckoned in
The thoughts I had that day!

But Cathy laughed and waved at them
From just beyond my reach,
And two of them came swimming and
They seized an ankle each,
They pulled her off the ledge and laughing
In that pool so blue,
Then swam around her teasing so
I knew not what to do.

Now Cathy was a swimmer, she
Could more than hold her own,
But when they swam around her
What I saw would make me groan,
For as they broke the surface I
Could see her face was pale,

And each of these fair maidens, well,
They had a fish's tail.

They whirled around and tumbled her
And pulled her by the hair,
And soon I saw her fighting them
As if in need of air,
I dived in then to free her but
They saw me coming down,
And took her to the depths with them
Until poor Cathy drowned.

I totally lost sight of them
And had to clamber out,
Sat weeping by the pool until
Just like a waterspout
Her body shot up from the depths
And then the mermaids three,
Swam clinging to each other, looked
Apologetically.

They didn't know we had to breathe
They had no need of air,
They made me signs of penance but
My Cathy simply stared,
And in her eyes a look of awe
As if in death she'd seen
A world that was worth dying for,
A dream within a dream.

The Egg

I'd thought that they were extinct until
I found one in the coop,
A genuine Jersey Giant, strutting
Up on the henhouse roof,
Twice the size of the other hens
As I said to my sister, Faye,
'Where did it come from?' She replied,
'Not there yesterday!'

'I go to collect the eggs each day,
Do you think that could be missed?
That bird is a giant,' she declared,
'So don't blame me, desist!'
I calmed her down, for she used to flare
At the slightest hint of crit.,
'Whatever it is, it's here to stay,
Perhaps we can breed from it?'

There wasn't a cockerel near the size
Of this random Jersey Black,
'It must have come visiting overnight,
I joked, 'from a neighbour's shack.'
She wandered into the henhouse and
From behind an empty keg,
She said, 'You'd better come look at this,'
And showed me a giant egg.

An egg so big that you wouldn't think
That a chicken could let it pass,
Tall and brown with a pointed crown
And a shell as thick as glass,

'Are we going to let it hatch it out,'
Said Faye, 'or crack it yet?
I wonder how many that would feed
As a giant omelette?'

'We'll leave her be, and we'll wait and see
If a monster's there inside,
We might as well, if a cockerel
It can be the henhouse pride.'
So we let her sit on the giant egg
For a week, or maybe more,
Then Faye came running inside one day,
'You've not seen this before!'

The egg emitted a humming noise
And rocked a bit on its base,
While through the shell there were coloured lights
That would fade then grow apace,
And as we stood it began to crack
Then pieces would fall away,
It almost gave me a heart attack
For what I saw that day.

For spinning inside the egg we saw
A tiny universe,
With a sun-like star at the centre and
Our planets, in reverse,
And as we watched it began to grow
To float out the henhouse door,
Swelling constantly as it rose
To the skies, with a mighty roar.

I don't know what it has done to us,
The sky doesn't look the same,

There are three moons now in the evening sky
Since the Jersey rooster came,
I lopped the chicken that laid the egg
And I wait for the slightest sight,
With an axe for the Jersey cockerel
That Faye prays to at night.

The Non-Event

We decided to offer a non-event
For it hadn't been done before,
We ordered a super, over-sized tent
And the grass to grow on the floor,
But the tent was cancelled the day it came
And the grass returned to the man,
For who ever heard of a non-event
That ever ran strictly to plan?

There are music events, and party events,
And horsey events, equine,
Racing events and crazy events
And lazy events, sublime.
There's events to do most anything
Which is why I thought it true,
That the most exciting event of the year
Would be one with nothing to do.

We'd offer an awesome Rock event
With a band who wouldn't be there,
And a totally gratis haircut, meant
For the men without any hair.
A skin tattoo for the motley crew
That we know as tits and tatts,

Then tell them the ink was really glue
For manufacturing hats.

The roads would be blocked for an hour or less
With the cars that never came,
We'd put the non-event posters up
They could read them all in vain.
I hear we're up for a Nobel Prize
For giving it up on Lent,
That one and only, never to come see
World Class Non-Event!

The Wake

We'd been at sea on a cruise ship,
Some days to Paradise,
An island in the pacific
Of beaches, trees and spice,
But storms, they were foregathering
Not just for the ship at sea,
For frost with us was travelling
Inside Caitlin and me.

With eyes averted we rarely spoke
There were demons in my head,
For she would flutter about at night
Not join me in our bed.
The ship ploughed on through a restless sea,
While the clouds outside were grey,
And I began to regret that we
Had chosen this holiday.

I woke each morning before the dawn
And not a word was said,
For Caitlin lay, facing away
On the far side of our bed.
I'd roam around in the early hours
The silent, deserted ship,
But a life aboard alone, it sours
By the fifth day of a trip.

The clouds grew dark, enveloped the ship
And mist lay deep on the decks,
While down beneath the fathomless sea
Lay a thousand sunken wrecks.
A thousand wrecks of hopes and dreams
That started away like this,
Lost forever beneath the sea
At the lack of a touch, or kiss.

We sailed, we sailed, by God we sailed
With our heartsick contraband,
For days we sailed as the storm winds railed
But we caught no sight of land,
We caught no sight of the what-we-were
Before, when our world was new,
For love was blind in the mist and wind
That sailed with the cruise ship too.

Surely there was a meeting point
Between the land and the sea,
But the ship sailed on with our tempers gone,
We sailed in misery,
A day beyond our arrival point
The Captain came to say,

'The land has gone, there's something wrong
We were due there yesterday.'

Wherever we looked about to see
The sea was all we saw,
I'd turn and spin, keep my hopes within,
All hope had flown before.
We cruise around in an endless sea
With never a sight of land,
And nothing is left of what was 'we'
It's buried in sea and sand.

Buried alive in the sea and sand
With a frost that shatters the eye,
Gone with the hope of sighting land
Between the sea and the sky.
We're drifting now, for we're out of fuel
In a world of liquid pride,
With she content at the prow of the ship
And I with the wake that died.

Thicker than Water

He sat in his favourite corner,
Each day, just taking his pills,
The old man, Frederick Horner
Counting his cash and paying his bills,
They watched and noted his every move,
Took note of each sign of life,
He'd outlived both of his daughters,
And even his scheming wife.

He never revealed how old he was
And nobody knew the truth,
He said he was old as Methusaleh,
Remembered the Biblical Ruth,
He still had the very first dollar he'd earned
Had framed it, and locked in his drawer,
But now he had multi-billions,
And each day added more.

'You'd think he would give us some,' they said,
His sons, Nathaniel and George,
For they had to work for their daily bread,
And Nathaniel slaved at a forge.
'He can't live forever,' George opined
'And then it will pass to us,'
The money was always on George's mind,
As he drove the local bus.

'We're not getting younger,' Nathaniel said,
'I'm forty and you're forty-two,
We could have made good if he'd shown some trust,
But look at our Becky and Sue.

They both died young, of neglect they said,
And mother, she died from the shakes,
But he goes on, he's just about dead,
It must be those pills he takes.'

They'd watched him taking his yellow pills,
He never said what they did,
The blue, kept under the windowsill,
The orange, the old man hid.
'It must be them that keep him alive,
The orange, the yellow and blue,
What if we take the pills away?'
'You can, but it's up to you.'

'Maybe we ought to try them first,
They could give us both long life.'
'They didn't do much for her,' said George,
'The old man's second wife.'
Nathaniel nodded and looked quite grim
He remembered the yellow pills,
Spilling out of the woman's hand
When she fell down, deadly ill.

They'd never been close to their father when
Their mother suddenly died,
Whenever there was an argument
They'd taken their mother's side,
The old man sat in his corner and
Would mutter of stains and blood,
Would wait for a glimmer of light to shine
But doubted they understood.

'We'll try the blue, one pill apiece
One night when he's in his bed,'

And so they did, they swallowed them down
In seconds they fell down dead.
The old man grinned in his final breath,
'Too curious, those two,
They should have asked who their father was
For it wasn't me… I knew!'

The Girl with a Deadly Charm

The first time that I noticed them
I passed them on the stair,
She wore an amulet love-charm then
He was much too old for her.
I should have hurried and looked away
But I caught her smouldering eye,
And my heart had leapt within my breast
To this day, I wonder why?

Her hair, a tangle of lovers knots,
Her lips, a definite pout,
Her figure light and her legs were white
And I saw her look about.
She peeked behind as she passed me by
And I caught her knowing look,
The moment passed with the slightest sigh
I was firmly on her hook.

I didn't go out of my way for her,
She seemed so firmly fixed,
The man beside her glowered at me
And gripped her by the wrist,
I saw him leading her often then
As our paths began to cross,

And smiled at her as she came my way
But her eyes looked vague, and lost.

The man came up and he gripped my arm,
'You'd better leave her be.
Don't think to fall for her fateful charm,
Giselle belongs to me!'
He pushed me then, and he walked away
And he gripped her arm so tight,
He stopped the blood where his fingers lay
And her hand went stark and white.

I asked a friend who had known her once,
He said, 'Just keep away.
She labours under a curse, that one,
She only brings dismay.
You see the man who escorts her now
And you think he's far too old,
A year ago he was twenty-two
But he aged once in her hold.'

I didn't think it was possible
But he aged as time went on,
His hair and his beard went pale and grey
And his features, pale and wan,
Though she gained colour in both her cheeks
And her eyes would sparkle blue,
While he would stumble, but still cling on
Till she said, 'I'm looking at you!'

As soon as she uttered those fateful words
His hand released its grip,
And she walked on, not looking back
As if on a different trip.

She came to face me and say the words
That had snared good men before,
But I turned into my passageway
Grey faced, and I locked the door.

The Village that Lived in the Sky

There's a village on top of a mountain
That's always surrounded by mist,
They have a miraculous fountain
Allowing the folk to exist,
And no-one remembers the world below
They think that they float in the void,
Their library holds a single book
Called something, 'According to Freud'.

They choose a new partner every night
In a version of musical chairs,
Nobody knows who belongs to who
And nobody really cares,
The women weave and the men deceive
In the way that it's been for years,
And then at night, they put out the light
And lie back, counting the stars.

They're trying to bottle the moonbeams,
To capture the secret of light,
And catch the sparkling frost that melts
Up on the mountain's height,
The day that a mountaineer appeared
Climbing up out of the mist,
They thought the devil had somehow reared
Out of his precipice.

The villagers gradually dwindled,
They died or they jumped right off,
He spoke to them in a different tongue
And they said that they'd had enough.
He tried in vain to explain again
That his name was Karsikov,
But the village slowly emptied out,
They thought that he'd said, 'Fuck off!'

Return of the Wanderer

There's a time at night when the moon is full
And the breakers pound the beach,
The world is dark and asleep, the gull
Lies nesting at the breach,
It's then that the stirrings from the depths
Reach out, like a dead man's hand,
And shortly, out of the rivulets
There are footprints on the sand.

They come ashore and they stand awhile
And they point, this way and that,
Considering well which way to go
As the waves erase their tracks,
Then a breeze picks up and it parts the grass
In a line up from the shore,
And the shape of feet on a farmer's stile
Are left, till they dry once more.

While up on the rise, a cottage sits
With a single faint night-light,

Its simple beam like a beacon streams
Through the tar-black pitch of night,
While deep inside in a cosy room
Sleeps a girl called Carolyn,
Who tosses fretfully in the gloom
As she dreams the words, 'Come in!'

The footsteps up from the field below
Stand still at the old front door,
The lock is rusty, the hinges swing
For an inch, or maybe more,
The wind is moaning and soughing now
And the door is soon ajar,
As the footsteps enter that sacred place
Under the evening star.

And Carolyn lies and moans aloud
As his death invades her sleep,
Since ever the depths had formed his shroud
All she had done was weep,
The footprints stood, facing her bed
For an age it seemed, they kept
A silent vigil, there by her head
When she woke, the sheets were wet.

I Wish I Could Be Like You!

Deep in the gloom of her bedroom,
Young Kathy dried her tears,
It wasn't as bad as the red room
She'd been banished to for years,
At least up there she could lie and dream
And play with her music box,
Not hear her parents arguing,
Whether they did, or not.

At least up here was her sanctuary
Where she could dream all day,
Of skipping out in the poppy fields
Where all the children play,
She'd lie there nursing a broken heart
For the loss of her former life,
For all had changed in her home, The Grange
When he took a second wife.

When her father took a second wife
And his face became so grim,
It seemed she couldn't do anything right
For the sake of pleasing him,
The woman snapped and the woman snarled
And she said to call her Ma,
But Kathy had kept her lips shut tight
That was just one bridge too far.

So she lay and opened the paste-board lid
And the dancer, up she leapt,
Straightening out her toutou as
She tried one pirouette,

With one hand up to her forehead and
The other fixed and set,
The dancer twirled in her private world
To a Mozart minuet.

And Kathy thought she was beautiful
As she balanced on her toes,
A look of grace on her tiny face
And the flush of love, it shows,
With glitter up in her auburn hair
And a spangle on each shoe,
The thought had formed as the doll performed,
'I wish I could be like you!'

'I wish I could be like you,' she thought
'So small, and full of grace,
I'd never have to go down again
With tears on my face,
I'd wait till somebody wound me up
Then I'd dance for them with pride,'
And something happened to Kathy then,
A change that she felt inside.

For all the while that the dancer twirled
To the Mozart minuet,
It took in Kathy's tear-stained face
And it seemed somewhat upset,
'Why should she have this lovely room
And a life that I'm denied,
I wish I could be like you,' it thought,
And the two thoughts did collide.

There seemed a change in the very air
Of that too secluded gloom,

When everything with bated breath had
Stopped in that fated room,
Then Kathy leapt to her feet with joy
And a final pirouette,
While the dancer smiled as at first she trialled
To that Mozart minuet.

The father arrived back home that night
To a scene of blood and gore,
His wife impaled with a table knife
Lay dead on the kitchen floor,
While Kathy twirled in the poppy fields
In a show of poise and grace,
And there in the bedroom, up above
There was blood on the dancer's face.

The Fisherman

He walked on up to the cottage from
The cliff, the long way round,
He didn't want to be seen or heard,
His footsteps made no sound,
He was wearing the same old overcoat
That he'd worn, those years before,
When he'd sauntered out of the cottage,
To take a walk on the shore.

The weather then had been brisk and cold
In the first few days of Spring,
The clouds had been light and fluffy then
He remembered everything,
The gulls were nested along the cliff
And the tide was on the turn,
A single fisherman cast his line
On the far side of the burn.

The pathway down by the cliff had been
Rock strewn and fairly steep,
His steps back then had been tentative,
He had time enough to keep,
He'd told his wife he'd be back by one
From his walk along the shore,
And she had blown him a kiss for fun
As she swept him out the door.

But now he looked at the garden that
Had been so nicely mown,
The privet hedge, the wisteria
Were all now overgrown,

The cottage needed a coat of paint
And the chimney pots were cracked,
He stopped and mused at the garden gate
For the love the cottage lacked.

Then a face appeared at the window that
Was pale, and sad, and drawn,
And he wished the earth would swallow him
From the day that he was born,
The door flew open and out she flew
Like a shrew, with little grace,
A look of scorn as he stood there, torn
And she slapped him round the face.

'What do you mean by coming here,
Did you hope to see my tears?
You walked away, not a word to say
And you don't come back for years.'
She screamed and pounded his overcoat
As he took one pace, and stepped,
Folding his arms around her as
She clung to him, and wept.

'I think I know how the others felt
But it's all beyond recall,
I only talked to the fisherman,
And I was held in thrall,
He talked and talked of the things to come
It was most distinctly odd,
The world closed in around me till
I felt I was talking to God.'

'He said so much, and it sounded wise
But I can't recall a thing,

I wanted to get back home to you
For time was hastening,
But the sun went down and the Moon came up
Which was when he said it, then,
'I'm not here looking for fish,' he said,
'For I'm a fisher of men.'

'It's been three years,' said his tear-stained wife,
'It has been three years or more,
Since ever you took your leave of me
To wander down on the shore.'
'That was the time of his ministry,'
He said, 'and I was to blame,
He kept on calling me Judas, though
I said that wasn't my name.'

'He said that we needed forgiveness, like
I need forgiveness from you,
I honestly don't know where I've been
But I know I've always been true.
He packed up his fishing tackle in
A bag he kept on the sand,
Took thirty pieces of silver
And placed them back in my hand.'

Goodbye!

There comes a day when a love that's frail
Will shatter at a touch,
No matter how long it's been that way
And has hung together, just,
The storm that gathers at eye and lip
Bursts out of a clear blue sky,

In a day of rage that will turn the page
And will leave you asking why?

The clouds will gather, the lightning strike
And the swift torrential rain,
Will tear apart an uncertain heart
And will douse your love with pain,
It matters not if you back away
Or appease a fevered mind,
For words are said that in truth are bled
From a feeling most unkind.

You're torn apart in a retrospect
Of the years you thought were fine,
But now discover that ancient lover
Was keeping tabs on time,
It seems that nothing was ever right
That you did in years before,
The cruel asides and the parting jibes
As they slam that final door.

It taints the best of your memories
It empties feelings inside,
It's like a war with an empty core
Lost in a sea of pride,
But even then when you can't pretend
That the end is worth a sigh,
The saddest sound in that dismal round
Is that final word, 'Goodbye!'

The Horror Tales of the Greats

He slipped on a set of headphones,
Adjusted a dial or two,
Then introduced his radio show
And the members of his crew,
'The Horror Tales of the Greats' he read
Each week to the folk in town,
Just as the Moon was coming up
With the sun then truly down.

And the folk had huddled round speakers
To hear, in a thousand homes,
The tales of Edgar Allan Poe
In the speaker's crackling tones,
And an eerie mist fell over the town
If they chanced to look outside,
As the ghosts of horror stories past
Rose up from the place they died.

Each tone was sent with a shiver
From the night's Plutonian shore,
Just as that stately bird of old
Had repeated, 'Nevermore!'
While the cats had yowled in the alleyways
When he read a tale of sin,
Of walling up the corpse of his wife
When the Black Cat did him in.

The Fall of the House of Usher,
The Masque of the Red Death,
The tales built up in the atmosphere
And made them short of breath,

The Cask of Amontillado,
The Pendulum and the Pit,
Whatever the horror, and most intense
There was always more of it.

The stars that shone in the evening sky
Had gone, though the sky was clear
As the Moon had dropped down, over a hill
While the airwaves dripped with fear,
And the walls back there, in the studio
Were seeming to seep a flood,
As the speaker droned in the microphone
The studio filled with blood.

And suddenly then, a different voice
Was heard all over the town,
Rattling through their radio's
And shouting the reader down.
'Shutter your windows and lock your doors
Put children under the bed,
Hide yourselves right under the stairs
Or you may well end up dead!'

'The very air that you breathe has been
Long saturated with dread,
Has filled your lungs with the ripe unclean
That came from somebody's head.
The ghostly voice on your radio
That has whispered blood and gore,
Will drown tonight in the studio
So there won't be any more.'

And right behind that terrible voice
There was choking sounds and screams,

Enough to curdle the very blood
And to give them nightmare dreams,
Then after a long, chilled silence of
The type that terror sates,
A voice said, 'that was the final of
The Horror Tales of the Greats.'

The Landslide

'There are times and tides in every life,
There are things we never planned,'
The old man said to his grandson there
As he took him by the hand,
'It may come soon, or it may come late,
It may be the final fall,
But when it does you may find you're left
With your back against the wall.'

The lad stood still on the rocky ledge
He was more than petrified,
For half the cliff had given way
In a sudden, great landslide,
The path that they had travelled on
Had plummeted into the bay,
There was no forward, and no way back
Where they stood on the cliff that day.

'Do you think they'll come to rescue us,
Do they even know we're here?'
The lad had cried in the first aside
Of his terror, and his fear,
The old man looked at the darkening light
And the clouds foretold a storm,

'I think that we'll be stranded here
All night, till the early morn.'

The old man looked where the cliff above
Had an overhanging ridge,
There was no way to clamber up
From their place on the narrow ledge,
And straight below, two hundred feet
Was the churn of an angry sea,
'I think we'll have to be more than brave
My boy, just you and me.'

The night came on with a swirl of wind
The first from an evening squall,
While they sat down on the narrow ledge
Their backs to the old cliff wall,
The lad was cold and his face was pale
So his grandpa held him tight,
'Just think of what you can tell your friends
Once back from this dreadful night.'

The rain that came was torrential,
They both were soaked to the skin,
He wrapped his coat all around the boy
But he felt him shivering,
'This brings back memories from the war
I was sat in an LCT,
Waiting for it to come and land
And to set the beaches free.'

The lad perked up, said, 'tell me more,
Did you find yourself afraid?'
'We knew the odds, we had gone to war
And the mines, they all were laid,

We hit the beach and they dropped the door
I was waist deep in the sea,
Trying to make it into shore
But I lived, and so can we!'

The boy was shivering constantly,
He'd die before the morn,
The old man struggled him to his feet,
'We have to get you warm!
We're both stood here in our LCT
And we're brave, our hearts are pumped...'
He turned and smiled at the lad, and then,
Holding hands, they jumped!

Index of First Lines

Alan had stood at our open door,	93
Back in the tiny town of Hamm	105
Deep in the gloom of her bedroom,	146
He came on down from the mountain like	20
He had got on the train at New Street,	91
He sat in his favourite corner,	139
He slipped on a set of headphones	153
He trudged on up from the great seaport	83
He walked on up to the cottage from	149
He wandered along the decks by night,	47
He was hanging in line with the elder trees	44
His parents had both been gone so long	58
His wife was due on the midnight plane	71
Houghton Hall had been derelict	96
I had an Indian Fakir come	88
I'd thought that they were extinct until	133
I have a man with a pointy hat	18
I like to walk on the beach, I said,	22
I'm hot on the tail of a poem's trail	108
I recall I lay at the top of the hill	27
Is it God out there in the woods tonight	56
It started when he had brought a box	74
It was always a hassle on Fridays	110
It was threatening rain for a week or more	65
I've had a terrible day today	31
I've kept a journal of sorts for years	116
I wanted to go to the end of the street	11
I was sat in a tavern in Pompey Town	9
I was sitting outside the house at dawn	118
'I would if I could but I can't,' he said,	67
I wrote a book called 'The Afterdeath'	103

Nadine was naive when she came to me	36
Rosalyn stood in the castle tower	85
She asked me how she had come to me	7
She didn't look awfully well that day	60
Some once called him a grand old man	69
The change in his habits was hard to define,	99
The Church in its awesome majesty	24
The first time that I noticed them	141
The Lady Mary had locked the door	51
The man had a terrible temper	16
The path that I like to wander on	42
'There are giants out in the hinterland,	77
'There are times and tides in every life,	155
There comes a day when a love that's frail	151
'There's a crafty witch in Willow Vale	126
There's an angel down in my garden plot	29
There's a time at night when the moon is full	144
There's a village on top of a mountain	143
The storm outside was abating, or	33
The sun had not even risen when	62
The three of us had been travelling	53
They lived in a farm on the lower slopes	123
They said it was only climate change,	80
They sat at the kitchen table as	113
The world looks grim when your eyes are dim	101
We came in through the undergrowth	120
We'd been at sea on a cruise ship,	136
We decided to offer a non-event	135
We had come across this grotto in	130
We never forget the ones we loved	129
We were swept up onto this rocky coast	39
What happens to love that's neglected	35
When Alison left the bath to run	13

www.ingramcontent.com/pod-product-compliance
Lightning Source LLC
Chambersburg PA
CBHW061654040426
42446CB00010B/1730